# Healing the Breach

# Mormonism, Metaphors, and the Pieces of the Puzzle

Patrick S. McKay, Sr.

Holy Scriptures, Translated and Corrected by the Spirit of Revelation, by Joseph Smith, Jr., the Seer, Published by The Church of Jesus Christ of Latter–Day Saints, Plano, Illinois, Joseph Smith, L.L. Rogers, E Robinson, Publishing Company, 1867.

The Book of Mormon, Translated by Joseph Smith, Jr. Compared with the Original Manuscript and the Kirtland Edition of 1837, which was carefully re-examined and compared with the Original Manuscript by Joseph Smith and Oliver Cowdery. Authorized Edition, Lamoni, Iowa Published by the Board of Publication of the Reorganized Church of Jesus Christ of Latter Day Saints, 1908.

ISBN: 978-1-4834-9096-0 (sc)
ISBN: 978-1-4834-9097-7 (hc)
ISBN: 978-1-4834-9079-3 (e)

Library of Congress Control Number: 2018910571

Lulu Publishing Services rev. date: 09/26/2018

# Healing the Breach

## Mormonism, Metaphors, and the
## Pieces of the Puzzle

**ZionBound.org**

**Biblical References**

From the King James Version,
unless notated as the Inspired Version (IV),
Holy Scriptures, Translated and Corrected by the Spirit of
Revelation by Joseph Smith, Jr., the Seer, Published by
The Church of Jesus Christ of Latter-Day Saints, Plano,
Illinois, Joseph Smith, L.L. Rogers, E. Robinson,
Publishing Company, 1867.

**Book of Mormon References**:

First reference RLDS Chapter and Verse,
The Book of Mormon, Authorized Edition, Lamoni, Iowa.
Published by the Board of Publication of the Reorganized
Church of Jesus Christ of Latter Day Saints, 1908.
Second Reference LDS Chapter and Verse.

**Doctrine and Covenants** (D&C):

First Reference RLDS Section and Verse,
Published by The Church of Jesus Christ of Latter-Day Saints,
Lamoni, Iowa, 1897.
Second Reference LDS Section and Verse,
The Church of Jesus Christ of Latter-day Saints, Salt Lake City,
Utah, 1974.
Third Reference BofC (A Book of Commandments),
Board of Publication, Church of Christ, Temple Lot,
Independence, Missouri, 1960.
(Roman numeral section numbers have been converted into
Arabic numerals.)

All quotes from Scriptures in this book have been italicized.

# Acknowledgements

I am grateful to Patti and Sariah Frye for their proofreading and editorial help. Thanks to Frank Frye for the layout, design and index; to Paul Mackender for his illustrations bringing life to the text, and to Becky Tarbuk for her untiring encouragement to persuade me to write, and to the faithful Saints I have been privileged to meet in the different branches of the Restored Church who are stirred by the dream of Zion. Finally, I thank my wife, Joy, for her unfailing love and constant support.

# Foreword

In the early days of the Restoration, differences finally prevailed and separated the first two elders of the nascent church, Joseph Smith and Oliver Cowdery. For ten years Oliver tried to make his way without the church and still maintain his belief in the Restoration. During this time, his brother-in-law, Phineas Young, diligently tried to bring him back into the fold. Eventually Phineas won out, and Oliver returned and was rebaptized.

Today in many ways, Patrick McKay, who belongs to the Restoration Branch Movement, is following the example of Phineas Young and doing all he can to try and heal the breaches in the original Restoration. For five years he has distributed an online, weekly newsletter, which has been dedicated to the reuniting of all the branches of the 1830 Restoration. For ten years he has been a driving force in holding yearly Book of Mormon conferences dedicated to strengthening belief in the Book of Mormon. Now Patrick is taking the next bold step and publishing a compilation of witnesses from various branches of the Restoration. His purpose is very transparent. He has committed himself to repairing the breach within Mormonism. His mantra (if not motto) could well be Isaiah 52:1, *"Awake, awake; put on thy strength, O Zion; put on thy beautiful garments."*

So he has gathered together the testimonies of diverse believers in the Restoration for the purpose of perspective. In this volume his intent is to build faith: faith in the Restoration, faith in the Book of Mormon, and faith in the gathering of the Saints back into one fold. Those who read this short anthology with eyes of faith are sure to feel a spirit of healing and share in Patrick's desire to hasten the day of reunion.

Keith Wilson
Associate Professor of Ancient History
Brigham Young University

# Prologue

There is a wisdom and a generosity in God the Father's exercise of His rule over His children. God has permitted the divisions of the Restoration just as he permitted the divisions of the house of Lehi into tribes. Through the divisions each facet of the Restoration has been able to manifest its own peculiar gifts in a way that opens blessings for all of us, if we permit it.

The various Restoration tribes have served to stir one another up and keep us in remembrance of our duty before God. Too often, however, we have busied ourselves in the task of defending our differences and preserving our borders more than we have considered our brethren and longed for a unified people with a singular focus of rejoicing and living in the peace which only Jesus Christ can establish. Patrick McKay is one of those who has considered the possibility of healing the wounds and bringing the tribes together.

*Healing the Breach: Mormonism, Metaphors and the Pieces of the Puzzle* is written to illustrate our God is not a respecter of persons and has been and is willing to bless all who will come to Him by faith in the name of Jesus Christ. Most commonly, the experiences and blessing of the people in the various Restoration groups intersect in the Book of Mormon.

The Book of Mormon is God's gift to the Gentiles and the Jews alike. It was planned, preserved and prepared for the latter-day age specifically and intentionally. The Book of Mormon is the vanguard of the work God is doing in the latter day to fulfill all the covenants He has made. We have all been made stewards of this work, but have not all been faithful in the execution of our stewardships. The testimonies of this book by Patrick McKay show God is faithful in His work with the Book of Mormon.

This book of testimonies presents a wide-angle view of the landscape of the Restoration as opposed to the narrow, focused view frequently held by many. From this broader perspective it is easy to observe the hand of God working in every group. Patrick's book draws our eyes to the work of God instead of our conflicts. This book should be a valuable tool helping to heal the breaches of the Restoration.

Gary Whiting
Quorum of Restoration Apostles
President

# Contents

# Introduction

*Behold, how good and pleasant it is for brethren to dwell together.*[1]

Have any of you ever attempted to put together a puzzle? If you look at the picture on the box out of which the puzzle came, you find the clues to begin putting the right pieces together. Typically, we work with a few pieces that match, and then we move outward looking for other parts that fit together. The actual solving of the puzzle is oftentimes a piecemeal process starting at one or more favorable places, continually linking the new fragments. The puzzle can be a mystery, and not unlike the various fractions of the Restored Church; the more parts there are, the greater the complexity. If, however, we see the picture on the box, we can find the necessary clues to begin the process of uniting the various pieces together. Our "keystone,"[2] the Book of Mormon, reminds us that *"there **are** save two churches only"*[3]—not that there will be, but that there *are* save two churches. For too long we have assumed that the only parts of the puzzle are those which are in our hands.

The God of Israel has been and continues to be active in sustaining His scattered and divided flock as we press forward toward the birth of Zion's redemption. The day is fast approaching when the compilation of the many testimonies manifest in the various branches of His church will be woven together into a beautiful tapestry revealing the effort of the Holy Spirit, that God might have a united people. The Saints in their "isolated churches" have only been disposed to view the backside of the tapestry. We have not been willing to turn it over to view its magnificence, leaving us instead to view the other parts of the Restoration (to which we do not belong) as nothing more than a jumbled mess of thread—all crisscrossed, frayed and knotted.

---

1    Psalm 133:1.
2    Statement by Joseph Smith, Jr., *History of the Church*, 4:461.
3    1 Nephi 3:220 [14:10], emphasis added.

This anthology of metaphors, joined with testimonies and divinatory expressions, is an *aide-mémoire* of the divine promise to the Scattered of the Restoration. It is written to disclose to its readers a glimpse of the rich colors, smooth texture and prophetic patterns of the numerous threads in the lives of all His Saints who have embraced the truth of the latter-day glory—making the textile of His Restored Church a thing of astonishing beauty. The Master Artisan is soon to reveal His finished product. The different fractions of the Restoration (the pieces of the puzzle) truly do fit together and are necessary to reach the intended goal of Zion, our picture on the box.

Patrick S. McKay, Sr.

# 1

# The Giant Redwoods

*And they did fellowship one with another, and did rejoice and did have great joy.[1]*

I grew up in California, where you find the giant redwoods, some of which tower over 350 feet into the air and are more than 2,500 years old. You would think they would possess an enormous root system extending hundreds of feet underground; but, actually, the roots on these giant sequoias are extremely shallow, no deeper than six to ten feet. So how do these massive trees stand a chance of staying upright, with all the winds which have blown upon them for all these years? Their secret is not in the depth of their roots but in their interconnected nature. Since the trees grow close together, their root systems become intertwined. So when the storms come and the winds blow, as they defiantly do in northern California, the giant redwoods stand strong because they're not standing

---

1     Helaman 2:121 [6:3].

alone. Each of them supports and protects the other. Additionally, these giant redwoods have bark up to three feet deep protecting the trees from fire damage.

What a great picture this portrays of our need for one another within the Restoration. We, the Saints, were designed just like the giant redwoods to grow together, not in isolation, but having our root systems intertwined, to provide mutual nourishment, protection, and support; and we cannot be so thin skinned that offenses will be able to divide us as a people.

The Restored Gospel finds its fulfillment in the redemption of Zion, the Holy City, where every man seeks the interest of his neighbor— doing all things with an eye single to the glory of God.[2] From one of the *Songs of Zion* we find these words:

> Oh Beautiful Zion our latter day theme,
> The prettiest picture, the loveliest dream.
> The prophets portrayed it that others might see
> And pass down the vision to you and to me.[3]

Have our eyes caught the vision, have our hearts felt the thrill? God's design is that the lives of the Saints should be characterized by this kind of interdependence, not merely in body but actively involved in sharing, giving, serving, learning and living together—becoming intertwined to behold the same vision of our latter-day theme.

We should discard the moniker of independent Restoration branches, or independent and isolated Restoration churches, and instead adopt the term interdependent Restoration branches/churches of the Restored Gospel. Our fellow believers in the Restored Gospel should

---

2   D&C 81:4g [82:19] Received September 1832.
3   *The Songs of Zion*, Arlene Buffington, Vol. 2, No. 177, "Oh Beautiful Zion." *The Songs of Zion* is a collection of hymns received by Sister Arlene Buffington by the Spirit of Revelation from the Church of Jesus Christ, (Bickertonite) over a period of more than forty years. These poetic and prophetic hymns have been plucked from the Tree of Life in the Paradise of God, testifying of our latter-day theme—Zion. (unpublished).

be our best friends. We should share one another's society, both in play and in worship. We should build and rebuild relationships on our commonalities. Friendships unite! When we consider our divine destiny as Saints of the latter days, our hearts are made glad by a foretaste of those joys which will be ours when we are gathered together into the Holy City. The Brother of Jared prayed for his *"friends;"* and God had compassion upon them, not confounding their language. King Benjamin addressed his people as *"my friends and my brethren."* In the testimony of John, Jesus said, *"Ye are my friends."* This, of course, is the model for our relationships one with another. The kingdom of God will be a kingdom of God's friends.

We know all too well that there are differences among the various parts of the Restoration; and these we have magnified, while failing to acknowledge and embrace our numerous commonalities. We all have the same mother, but were separated at birth, so to speak, following the death of Brother Joseph Smith, Jr. Since that time, we have become skilled and quite expert in dividing ourselves and standing aloof one from another, while the world waits and cries out for the manifestation of the sons of God. We need accountability and encouragement from one another if we expect to stand tall like the giant redwoods. It's not an option, but rather a matter of survival.

There are more than seven billion people in this world. Those who embrace the Book of Mormon are so few; the majority of the children of men know nothing of the Restored Gospel, but the adversary certainly does. The enemy has attacked the Restoration since 1830, and the Saints have been scattered. There are true and dedicated believers residing among all the fractions of the original church. The Holy Spirit resides with many, regardless of the organization they worship in. These separate fellowships are barriers, which have kept us divided. We cannot sew ourselves back together, but the Holy Spirit can and will.

Are we interconnected with fellow believers in the Book of Mormon and its message to restore the covenants He made with the house of Israel and gather them to Christ, to His doctrine, and to the lands of their inheritance? The Saints can continue the same old mantra of who has authority, whose administrative structure is pure and whose is flawed. Imagine with me for just a moment. If the Lord Jesus were to walk among us, inviting each of us to follow Him, I believe we all would arise and follow Him. If we did, do you realize all the differences we now have would no longer exist? He said, *"There shall be no disputations among you as there hath hitherto been."*[1]

We have the opportunity to enrich the soil for the Lord to sow that seed into our lives. And when that kernel sprouts, we will all see eye to eye. When the Lord moves, we will all be surprised and amazed. We will discover we all saw only a portion of the whole picture. Here is another quote from one of the poetic and prophetic *Songs of Zion*:

> God opened the door and the day walked in,
> We've heard for years you were on the way,
> Well, what do you know, today's the day.[2]

Can common activities and shared events change us, drawing us closer together to stir and motivate us to make that type of preparation that will allow our roots to become intertwined like the giant redwood trees? We all sing, preach, pray, yearn, and long for Zion. Yet no portion of the Restored Church has been able to complete this divine task assigned to the Saints to gather Israel and build the Holy City. In fact, it has now passed out of our hands. Zion will now be redeemed with judgment (that is the land) and her converts (the Saints) with righteousness.[3] Are we prepared? An awful storm is on its way. How well prepared will we be when it arrives? Prophetic counsel came to the Reorganized Church through Joseph Smith III many years ago to help the Saints approximate the Zionic ideal of blending our lives together:

> *So far as you can agree work together without heat, confusion, or malice .... Let nothing separate you from each other and the work*

---

1    3 Nephi 5:29 [11:28].
2    *The Songs of Zion*, Arlene Buffington, Vol. 2 No. 175, "The Day Walked In."
3    Isaiah 1:27.

*whereunto you have been called; and I will be with you by my Spirit and presence of power unto the end. Amen.*[4]

The message imbedded within this monograph is not asking any of the Saints to leave the place where God has planted them. Each church of the Restoration believes it represents the best or in some instances the only true expression of the latter-day work. No attempt will be made to challenge that belief. What is intended is to create an environment where fellowship centering on our common belief in the Book of Mormon can be fostered. Can we work together as far as possible to build genuine trust and respect and let God do the heavy lifting? May we see Him at work repairing the breach and restoring the pathways where our fathers walked so long. He beckons to us, "Come, Saints, build the old waste places," and "raise the old foundations high. Then our heritage will find us and our songs will fill the sky."[5]

------------------

*And he said unto me, Behold, there are save two churches only.*[6]

§

### The Manifestation of the Gift of Tongues

*And there appeared unto them cloven tongues like as of fire, and it rested upon each of them. And they were all filled with the Holy Ghost, and began to speak with other tongues, as the Spirit gave them utterance. And there were dwelling at Jerusalem Jews, devout men, out of every nation under heaven. Now when this was noised abroad, the multitude came together, and were confounded, because that every man heard them speak in his own language. And they were all amazed and marveled, saying one to another, Behold, are not all these which speak Galileans? And how hear we every man in our own tongue, wherein we were born?*[7]

------------------

4    D&C 122:16a, 17b.
5    *The Songs of Zion*, Arlene Buffington, Vol. 2, No. 210, "Lend the Weary Ones a Song."
6    1 Nephi 3:220 [14:10].
7    Acts 2:3–8.

5

## Testimony of Leonard Lovalvo
### As Told by his Grandson Leonard Lovalvo
### The Church of Jesus Christ (Bickertonite)

My grandfather came to the United States from his home in Italy. He did not speak any English. Several years after coming to the United States, my father invited him to attend church with him; but being of another faith, he refused every invitation. My father knew that the preaching would be in English and that he would not understand, but he invited him nonetheless. After many invitations, my grandfather decided to attend to a Sunday service at The Church of Jesus Christ.

My grandfather sat very attentively during the service without saying a word. After the service was over, he asked my father, "Why did you say that the service would be in English?" My father replied that the sermon was, in fact, delivered in English. Grandfather then declared "I heard the entire sermon in Italian." As a result, Grandfather began to attend church regularly.

One Sunday he saw Jesus Christ on the pulpit and He spoke to my grandfather saying, "*Leonardo, vieni, vieni* (Leonard, come, come)."

Following that service, my grandfather asked for baptism.

This is just a marvelous example of God's ability to stretch the boundaries of our human limitations. The generations of this family are still active in The Church of Jesus Christ today.[8]

### Brother Glenn Scott
### The Reorganized Church of Jesus Christ of Latter Day Saints

My mother's parents were both Holland Dutch. My grandmother grew up in Amsterdam in a fairly wealthy family. My grandfather grew up in a small town on the east side of what used to be called the Zuiderzee, in a little town called Meppel. He was Dutch Protestant, and my grandmother

---

8    Personal correspondence.

was Catholic. Since neither of their families was very enthusiastic about each other's religion, the couple decided to come to America to start their new married life in a new land. So they got on a sailboat and came to the United States. It was a long trip under sail—close to a month.

My grandmother was unusual for a European lady. She had a college degree and spoke six languages, but it just happened that none of them were English. She used to pray in Latin; she would think out her problems in German; of course, she spoke Dutch conversationally. I'm not sure how she knew Spanish, French, and Italian, but she spoke all of those.

As they were crossing the Atlantic at a very leisurely pace, they had time heavy on their hands. It happened that there was a Reorganized Latter Day Saint apostle named James Caffall on the ship, and he was presenting a series of missionary meetings. They didn't have anything else to do, so out of curiosity they went down to see what was going on.

Neither my grandmother nor my grandfather spoke any English at that time, and Apostle Caffall did not speak Dutch. But to their utter amazement, they understood every word he said. They recognized this as a miracle because they didn't know English, yet they understood all of his sermons. When they landed in the New World, they, with Apostle Caffall's help, immediately went to the nearest RLDS congregation and were baptized.[9]

---

*And it came to pass that the Lord of the vineyard said again unto his servant, Look hither, and behold another branch also, which I have planted; behold that I have nourished it also, and it hath brought forth fruit.*[10]

---

9   Transcription of an audio recording made from Glenn Scott, Palenque Press, July 6, 2001.
10   Jacob 3:67 [5:24].

# 2

# A Fortunate Fall

*Adam fell that men might be.*[1]

A while back I had a conversation with a BYU professor, who asked, "Patrick, do you believe in a fortunate fall?" I responded in the affirmative. Father Lehi taught, *"If Adam had not transgressed, he would not have fallen"* and he and Eve *"would have remained in a state of innocence, having no joy, for they knew no misery; doing no good, for they knew no sin."*[2]

St. Augustine and John Calvin both taught the doctrine of original sin, leaving mankind in a condition of total depravity without free will, unless predestined or elected by God to choose Him through prevenient

---

1    2 Nephi 1:115 [2:25].
2    2 Nephi 1:111 & 113, [24:10 & 12].

grace. The Book of Mormon clearly teaches that the Spirit of Christ, *"is given to every man, that they may know good from evil."*[3] It instructs us that the effects of the fall on our first parents must be viewed through Jesus' substitutionary death and the power of the atonement:

> *My Father sent me that I might be lifted up upon the cross; and after that I had been lifted up upon the cross; I might draw all men unto me.*[4]

The professor then began speaking to me of a reoccurring image presented to his mind: "Could the scattering of the Saints following the death of Joseph Smith, Jr., be a fortunate scattering?"

The children of Israel had been scattered and *"sifted among all nations, like as corn is sifted in a sieve"*[5] that God might preserve them unto Himself in the latter days, grafting the various plantings or branches back into the mother tree. If Zenos' parable applies to the house of Israel, why couldn't it apply to the Scattered of the Restoration? Nephi reminds us that we can *"liken all scriptures unto us that it might be for our profit and learning."*[6]

The comparison suggests that the time has come to begin tearing down the walls and begin building bridges among the Saints of the Restoration. Following the martyrdom of Joseph, steps were taken that led the various branches of the Restored Church to sew their organizations a bit differently. But enough time has elapsed—it is time now to take the cross-stitch, (or the bias), and suture us back together. The Restoration churches have each assumed the cross-stitch is not any good, that other parts of the Restoration do not stand in the light as "we" do; however with the bias, we are able to take the garment and make it strong, pliable, and fitted for the use for which it was intended or designed. If you look at a piece of felt, it is flat; there is no bias and it is not very pliable and can easily tear. God is in the process of taking the differences in the Restoration—the bias, if you like—and binding us

---

3     Moroni 7:14, [7:16] emphasis added.
4     3 Nephi 12:26, [27:14].
5     Amos 9:9.
6     1 Nephi 6:5, [19:23].

together that the gospel message can easily cover and protect the Saints, while also making them pliable, that we no longer will lament the fact that we have not been able to produce the kingdom of Zion.

There are many within the fabric of the Restoration who have the testimony of the latter-day light. It is God's purpose to now begin to unite us that we might accomplish the thing He has called us to do, that we might witness the completion of His *"strange act."*[7] There remains that haunting scripture given in the very early days of the Restoration, *"If ye are not one, ye are not mine."*[8]

Fruit trees cross-pollinate. We need to know that they require another tree for pollination—not just one of the same variety, but a different variety of the same fruit. These fruit trees need to blossom at the same time so the honeybees can cross-pollinate them. What a marvelous portrait sewn into nature revealing the process God intends for His most precious fruit, His Saints, the Scattered of the Restoration. Remember, we all have the same mother; but we were separated at birth. The churches of the Restoration are simply different varieties of the same fruit—they can and should be used to help cross-pollinate the fruit of the kingdom of God.

———————————

*Now, if we had not grafted in these branches, the tree thereof would have perished.*[9]

§

## Make Ready

*And now behold, I ask of you, my brethren of the church, Have ye spiritually been born of God? Have ye received his image in your countenances?*[10]

---

7    Isaiah 28:21, D&C 92:1c, [101:95], *The Evening and the Morning Star*, Vol. 1, No. 8, p. 61 (Jan. 1831).
8    D&C 38:6a [38:27]. Received January 2, 1831.
9    Jacob 3:56 [5:18].
10   Alma 3:27–28 [5:14].

## Dream of Sister Deb Haines
## The Church of Christ (Temple Lot)

I was in an off-white room, with a group of young children. It felt like a church basement, in a corner area, which was used as a nursery school. I saw young children and books, but there were no toys. It seemed as if it had become a study area/classroom instead. The children were gathered around me when I realized that someone had taken the changing table out of the area. I asked, "Where did it go?"

The voice of the Lord answered, "You no longer need it. They're not babies anymore."

I was instructed to bring in a low table and a mirror. The voice of the Spirit told me that the children should look in the mirror to see who they are (examine themselves), that they can fix their hair (prepare) and adorn themselves (with righteousness and charity). These things were impressed upon me ... they are to prepare to be the Bride of Christ. I then awoke.

Just after writing my dream, I checked our e-mail and noticed there was a Ladies' Circle newsletter from the Church of Jesus Christ (Bickertonite). I opened it and saw the title was "The True Reflection." There was a sketch of a woman sitting at a low table in front of a mirror like the one in my dream.[11] The article speaks of preparing to show God's reflection. This, to me, was a witness of the truth of the dream I had been given that very morning.

Just after typing my testimony of this dream, a song came to my mind. I began to hear it over and over, until I decided I needed to look it up in our hymnal. As I looked it up and I began reading, "One Day When Fell the Spirit's Whisper,"[12] the words in the beginning of the second verse hit me—"Sweet fell the call for Zion's children."[13]

---

11  October 30, 2012 Ladies' Circle Blog | Guest Blogger, Church of Jesus Christ (Bickertonite).

12  Audentia Anderson, granddaughter of Joseph and Emma Smith, "One Day When Fell the Spirit's Whisper," *The Hymnal*, #508, Herald Publishing House, Independence, Missouri, 1956.

13  Personal correspondence.

# Commentary

I t is remarkable and wonderful to tell that the "sweet call for Zion's children" is a call to examine ourselves and prepare for the Wedding Supper, clothing ourselves in righteousness with the bonds of charity, that *"when he shall appear we shall be like him."*[14] It is remarkable to hear that a dream which is received by a member of the Church of Christ (Temple Lot), finds a confirmation of that dream in a *Ladies' Circle* publication from the Church of Jesus Christ (Bickertonite), and an additional witness is given in the singing of the words of a hymn written by Vida E. Smith (from the RLDS Church—Josephites), granddaughter of Joseph the Martyr. From three separate branches of the Restoration comes once again the "Spirit's Whisper" to His scattered and divided flock, to make ready for the Bridegroom. The time for playing is over!

---

*Wherefore the voice of the Lord is unto the ends of the earth, that all that will hear may hear; prepare ye, prepare ye for that which is to come, for the Lord is nigh; and the anger of the Lord is kindled, and his sword is bathed in heaven, and it shall fall upon the inhabitants of the earth; and the arm of the Lord shall be revealed.*[15]

---

14   1 John 3:2, Moroni 7:53 [7:48].
15   D&C 1:3a–b [1:11–14]. *The Evening and the Morning Star*, Vol. 1 No. 10, March 1833. Revelation received on November 1, 1831.

# 3

# Mutualism

*And it came to pass that we went down to the land of our inheritance, and we did gather together our gold, and our silver, and our precious things.*[1]

Amutualistic relationship is when two organisms of different species work together, each benefiting from the relationship. Hundreds of examples of these symbiotic relationships exist in nature. The shrimp digs and cleans a burrow in the sand where both the shrimp and the goby fish live. The shrimp is almost blind and vulnerable to predators. The goby fish touches the shrimp with its tail to warn it of impending danger, and both shrimp and goby fish quickly retreat into the burrow for safety.

Bees fly from flower to flower, gathering nectar, which they make into food, benefiting the bees. When they land in a flower, the bees get pollen on their hairy bodies; and when they move to the next flower, some pollen rubs off, fertilizing the plant. In this interdependent relationship, the bees eat and the plants reproduce.

---

1    1 Nephi 1:85 [3:22].

Another example is seen in a small bird called the oxpecker, which lands on the rhino or zebra and eat ticks and other parasites that live on their skin. The oxpecker gets food, and the rhinos and zebras get pest control. Moreover, when there is danger, the oxpecker flies away screaming a warning, which helps protect these larger animals.

We see the same type of benefits exist among the Scattered of the Restoration. The Saints who have been raised with a little different legacy have acquired distinct traits and talents within their branches of the church, which the other branches can benefit from. Certain of these organizations are blessed with the outpouring of various gifts of the gospel, such as tongues, prophecy, dreams, visions, and the beholding of angels. Others possess great organizational skills to maintain balance, growth, and stability, while some have produced scholars who plumb the depths of the Scriptures to unmask hidden truths. Some are very structured, while others are more dynamic. But each has a benefit for the other.

Outside of the Restoration, our detractors have combined, attempting to discredit our message—finding a measure of success because they utilize their various strengths against the divided believers in the angel message. Even our smaller branches of the Restoration—like the oxpecker—can enrich the larger portions of the Church benefiting from our mutualistic association, where we can be alerted to the impending dangers by sharing valuable prophetic insights. The time has arrived for our individual strengths to be used to complement the others, as God prepares to bring judgment on our nation and at the same time vindicate the Restoration.

---

"The cause of God is one common cause, in which the Saints are alike all interested.... The advancement of the cause of God and the building up of Zion is as much one man's business as another's."[2]

---

2    Joseph Smith, Jr., *History of the Church* [LDS] Vol. 4 p. 609.

# §

## The Fierce Winds

*Go through, go through the gates; prepare ye the way of the people.*[3]

### Dream Received by Brother Merlin Eddy
### The Church of Christ (Temple Lot)

The scene in my dream was a vast expanse of clear ice. The ice was smooth and had no snow cover. Crossing this expanse of ice was a line of people. I could not determine who any of these people were; but I could see that there were men and women, both young and old. Those whom I saw were slowly walking in a single straight line, as if there was a path across the ice. All the people on the path were carrying or pulling luggage. There were groups that seemed to be family members and friends, as I could hear some talking and laughing. I could not see the beginning of the line or any edge of the expanse of the ice, as it was beyond my sight. The destination of this line of people was a large rock island that I could see in the distance. On this rock island was built a structure that looked like a castle made of stone.

Suddenly, and without warning, a fierce wind blew across the line of people. The people were being blown off the path, as there was no traction on the ice. A few in the line were prepared; and as the wind started to blow, they let go of the luggage they had and lay face down on the ice. Those who were prepared cried out to the others to let go of their luggage and lie flat on the ice so the wind would not sweep them away. Some lay on the ice but would not let go of their luggage; and as the wind caught the luggage, they continued to be blown off the path. Others were trying to crouch and walk into the wind, but they were blown off the path faster. I could hear screaming and crying for those who would not listen because they continued being swept off by the fierce and steady wind.

---

3     Isaiah 62:10.

Those who were prepared for the wind had two picks, one in each hand, which they plunged into the ice and could hold themselves in place. Some held on to those with the picks, and they were not swept away. I could see that some were close enough to the island that they could hold onto the rock outcroppings and hold fast against the wind. But all of those that would not obey the cries of those who were prepared, and the cries of the obedient, were swept off until they were out of sight. They would not let go of their luggage and lie down on the ice. There was much sorrow for the friends and family members who were swept off by the fierce and steady wind that suddenly swept across the path.[4]

---

## The Scarlet Thread

*But unto you that fear my name, shall the Son of righteousness arise with healing in his wings; and ye shall go forth and grow up as calves of the stall.*[5]

## Brother Dominick Scala
## The Church of Jesus Christ (Bickertonite)

A few weeks after I obeyed the gospel, my entire family was healed from an affliction. My wife, seven children, two grandchildren, and I were sick with scarlet fever. The board of health had quarantined our house. Because of this action, we were not able to attend the Sunday service. Our absence became apparent, and the brothers and sisters came to our home. Disregarding the quarantine sign that was posted, they came in and offered prayers on our behalf. Brother Louis Mazzeo anointed eleven of us. One by one, we arose from our beds, healed from scarlet fever. We thank God for such great power and healings.[6]

---

4    *History of the Church of Christ* (Temple Lot), Vol. 2, pp. 508–509.
5    3 Nephi 11:23 [25:2].
6    *A History of the Church of Jesus Christ* [Bickertonite], Vol. 2, p. 336.

## Sister Jane Couser
## The Reorganized Church of Jesus Christ of Latter Day Saints

I desire to give my testimony to the truth of this work. I know it is of God and that signs follow them that obey. I have seen them made manifest in my own house, for I have been healed. The doctor said I could not live but only a few hours. I was instantly healed through the administration of Brother Rathbun. My little girl was very low with scarlet fever. She was so far gone that we lifted her eyelids, and there was not one twitch of the eye. About one hour after she was administered to she began to move, and she got well.[7]

## Sister Betsey Smith
## The Church of Jesus Christ of Latter-day Saints

O n the third day of the beautiful month of May, in 1856, we embarked on the ship *Thornton*, from Liverpool, England, leaving the steam loom mills, the shores of Great Britain, our beloved native land, and dear old Scotland, for the gospel's sake. After six or seven weeks' sailing, seasickness, and stormy weather, we landed in New York City, and registered at the Castle Garden; in a few days we reached Iowa by rail. There we camped for weeks, waiting for the handcarts to be completed for the journey. While there, I was so sick with scarlet fever that I could not open my eyes. I heard Sisters Henderson and McPhail say, "I am sorry she is dying; another death in camp soon!" One baby had just died. I seemed to know that they were speaking of me. And when Mother came in from the campfire, with warm broth, she saw the tears in my eyes. "Are you worse?" she asked me. "Mother, they think I am dying; I want to live and go to the Valley." My dear mother, at that time in her fifty-second year, then went and brought the elders, who

---

7   *The History of the Reorganized Church of Jesus Christ of Latter Day Saints,*
    Vol. 4, p. 660.

administered to me and rebuked the disease, commanding it to leave both the camp and me. My recovery was rapid.[8]

---

# Commentary

We see through the prism of our histories the divine continuity of God's manifold grace extended to His scattered and divided flock. Each portion of the Restoration has been the recipients of this grace to confirm the authenticity of the work as well as sustain the Saints in their wilderness, as we await the day when the desert blossoms like a rose. In spite of some varied beliefs associated with the different branches of the latter-day work, the God of Israel has been mindful of each and will make all the wrongs right as He rises up to maintain His kingdom.

There have been and continue to be whisperings from across the Restoration to prepare the Saints for that which is to come. These prophetic breathings remind us that the angel has flown through the midst of heaven and restored the gospel, that those who embrace this message might escape the judgments foretold. Are we willing to let go of our possessions and positions and humble ourselves that we might not be swept off the path to Zion? The fierce winds are already beginning to blow upon this land to remove the iniquity and all things that offend, that His kingdom may emerge. Can we let go of our baggage that distracts us from holding firm to the rod of iron? May we, the Scattered of the Restoration look for opportunities to join together, helping the Saints prepare for that which is to come.

The promise of a deliverer, coupled with additional records to come forth, should assure us all that God is able to do His own work. Let us continue to build bridges on our commonalities as we wait upon Him

---

8    "The Tired Mother: Pioneer Recollections," by Mrs. Betsey Smith Goodwin, *Improvement Era*, July 1919, p. 775.

to bring clarity and purpose when He makes bare His arm to heal the breach and complete the Marvelous Work and a Wonder.

———————————

*Thy watchmen shall lift up the voice; with the voice together shall they sing, for they shall see eye to eye, when the Lord shall bring again Zion.*[9]

———————————

9    3 Nephi 7:43 [16:18].

# 4

# Cut Her Loose

*And it came to pass that the Lord spake unto me, saying, Thou shalt construct a ship, after the manner which I shall shew thee, that I may carry thy people across these waters.*[1]

$S$ everal years ago I read the front-page story in the *San Francisco Chronicle* about a female humpback whale that had become entangled in a spider web of crab traps and lines. She was weighted down by hundreds of pounds of traps that caused her to struggle to stay afloat. She also had hundreds of yards of line rope wrapped around her body—her tail, torso, and line wrapped around her mouth. A fisherman spotted her just east of the Farralone Islands (outside the Golden Gate) and radioed an environmental group for help. Within a few hours, the

1    1 Nephi 5:70 [17:8].

rescue team arrived and determined that she was so bad off, the only way to save her was to dive in and untangle her—a very dangerous proposition. One slap of the tail could kill a rescuer.

They worked for hours with curved knives and eventually freed her. When she was liberated, the divers say she swam in what seemed like joyous circles. She then came back to each and every diver, one at a time, nudging and pushing him or her gently around—she was thanking them. Some said it was the most incredibly beautiful experience of their lives. The individual who cut the rope out of her mouth related that her eye was following him the whole time, and he will never be the same.

This was an incredible story involving the rescue of a tangled whale by individuals who cared enough to invest their time, energy, and talent—as well as their safety—to free this marine creature from the snares that entangled her. The Ship of Zion, like the humpback whale in our story, is also entangled and unable to carry her fair sons and daughters safely to Zion's shore. Our latter-day hope stands in need of rescuing. Our Ship of State needs all hands on deck working in unison to cut her loose. The God of Israel in His mercy has prophetically forecast His intention to untangle the Saints, redeem Zion, and make a refuge for Israel that they might return with gratitude, singing songs of everlasting joy. This is our birthright, our future, and our divine destiny.

### Set Her Free

The cable strains the anchor resting on the ocean floor,
The earth begins to shake and break apart from shore to shore;
The howling wind relays to earth a message from the Lord,
If any care to live tonight, be quick to get on board.

The ship some call Old Zion and some call her Liberty,
The Ancient One, the Beautiful, the Vessel of the Free;

She takes her weary travelers to the regions of the blest,
For there the Motherland prepares a place where they can rest.

The morning breaks the eastern sky, the sunshine strains to see,
The wind fills up her lovely sails and sets the great ship free;
The Motherland is crying out, I'm clean at last, from sin,
So sail to me, Oh Mighty Ship, and bring my people in.

### Chorus

Cut her loose, for she's been tied too long.
Set her free, her destiny to catch the rising dawn.
And oh, the Motherland is weeping for the great ship's safe return,
As cities all across this land catch fire and start to burn.[2]

---

*Remember and keep the commandments, be alert to keep out of the church and from its members those forces, which make for disunity, and in harmony and saintly accord be about the task of freeing Zion from her bondage.[3]*

§

## Healed By God

*And they were healed by the power of the Lamb of God.[4]*

### Brother Russell M. Nelson
### The Church of Jesus Christ of Latter-day Saints

Many of us have had experiences with the sweet power of prayer. One of mine was shared with a stake patriarch from southern Utah. I first met him in my medical office more than 40 years ago, during the early pioneering days of surgery on the heart. This saintly soul suffered much because of a failing heart. He pleaded for help, thinking that his condition resulted from a damaged but repairable valve in his heart.

---

2   Arlene Buffington, *The Songs of Zion,* Vol. 1, No. 109, "Set Her Free."
3   Revelation received by President F. M. Smith of The Reorganized Church of Jesus Christ of Latter Day Saints, April 7, 1938, D&C 137:6a.
4   1 Nephi 3:85 [11:31].

Extensive evaluation revealed that he had *two* faulty valves. While one could be helped surgically, the other could not. Thus, an operation was *not* advised. He received this news with deep disappointment. Subsequent visits ended with the same advice. Finally, in desperation, he spoke to me with considerable emotion:

Dr. Nelson, I have prayed for help and have been directed to you. The Lord will not reveal to me how to repair that second valve, but He can reveal it to you. Your mind is so prepared. If you will operate upon me, the Lord will make it known to you what to do. Please perform the operation that I need, and pray for the help that you need.

His great faith had a profound effect upon me. How could I turn him away again? Following a fervent prayer together, I agreed to try. In preparing for that fateful day, I prayed over and over again, but still did not know what to do for his leaking tricuspid valve. Even as the operation commenced, my assistant asked, "What are you going to do for that?"

I said, "I do not know."

We began the operation. After relieving the obstruction of the first valve, we exposed the second valve. We found it to be intact but so badly dilated that it could no longer function, as it should. While I examined the valve, a message was distinctly impressed upon my mind:

"Reduce the circumference of the ring."

I announced that message to my assistant. "The valve tissue will be sufficient if we can effectively reduce the ring toward its normal size."

But how? We could not apply a belt as one would use to tighten the waist of oversized trousers. We could not squeeze with a strap, as one would cinch a saddle on a horse. Then a picture came vividly to my mind, showing how stitches could be placed—to make a pleat here and a tuck there—to accomplish the desired objective. I still remember that mental image—complete with dotted lines where sutures should be placed. The repair was completed as diagrammed in my mind. We tested the valve and found the leak to be reduced remarkably. My assistant said, "It's a miracle."

I responded, "It's an answer to prayer."

The patient's recovery was rapid and his relief gratifying. Not only was he helped in a marvelous way, but also surgical help for other people with similar problems had become a possibility. I take no credit. Praise goes to this faithful patriarch and to God, who answered our prayers. This faithful man lived for many more years and has since gone to his eternal glory.[5]

### Brother Joseph Smith, III
### The Reorganized Church of Jesus Christ of Latter Day Saints

The years 1878 and 1879 were years of trouble for the branch of the Reorganized Church in Plano, Illinois. There was considerable sickness among all classes of people, due to typhoid. Although the branch was quite large, only three or four elders were available for visiting the sick as the law provides. One thing that seemed to annoy these elders was that physicians were employed. Sometimes, both doctors and elders would be found at the bedside of the sick at the same time or following each other at intervals. Over the weeks this became irksome, though none of the patients seemed to complain. They seemed satisfied, and not many died.

One night at the close of a long tedious day, a good part of which was spent in going from place to place visiting and administering to the sick, Joseph Smith III after consulting with the other elders concluded that he would refuse to go to places where a physician had been employed. He justified himself with the saying: "They appeal to medicine; let them take the benefit of their appeal or suffer the consequences." With this conclusion he went to bed.

---

5   LDS General Conference, 2003.

That evening he was visited by a messenger who began to interview him:

"Some of those to whom you are called have physicians attending them also?"

Joseph replied, "Yes sir. Some do not care to trust to administration of the elders alone."

The messenger with a twinkle in his eye then said, "You elders seem not to like this."

"No sir, we do not."

"You think that those who are sick should be satisfied with either the doctors or the elders and ought not to call on both?"

Joseph rejoined, "Yes, we think it a little inconsistent to rely or seem to rely on both."

This interview with the messenger went on for some time. Then he posed another question to Brother Joseph. "By what power," he asked, "is the healing of the sick by the laying on of hands by the elders wrought? Is it by the power of God, or is it because of some goodness or power in you elders?"

Joseph replied, "It is by the power of God."

The messenger continued, "Well, then, believing as you say you do—that the power by which the healing is done is the power of God; and that in each instance where administration is had, whether the elders alone are called or a doctor is also called, the healing power is sent or withheld according as it is decided by the wisdom of God—do you not think that it is your duty, the duty of the elders who believe and teach the doctrine of the laying on of hands, to go when called, administer according to such belief and teaching, and leave the matter in God's hand to send the power and heal or otherwise as He may in His wisdom decide, whether a doctor has been called or not?"

Joseph again answered, "Well, yes; I suppose so."

The messenger concluded by saying, "I think so, too. Good night!"

From that day forward, whenever Joseph Smith III was called to administer for the sick, he never again questioned or cared whether a doctor had been called or the elders alone. He believed the visitation of the heavenly messenger was sent to teach him his duty (and the elders generally) in the manner of administration to the sick and suffering regardless if the faith in them who were anointed was weak or strong.[6]

---

# Commentary

Alma reminds us that when the Nephites were faced with fevers, they were blessed because of the quality of the many plants and roots, which God had prepared to remove the cause of disease.[7] Modern medicine has been able to recruit many of these plants in our day to provide relief to millions of people. Additionally, God has placed within the fabric of the Restored Church various helps and governments to bless, comfort, sustain, and succor His people, including the laying on of hands for the restoration of health. Many Saints from the various churches of the Restoration can testify of the efficacy of this ordinance. These testimonies reveal that God presides over the issues of life and has at His disposal various and sundry ways in which He can provide relief to the Saints that they might *grow up as calves of the stall*" [8] and give God the glory, which rightly belongs to Him. Even as God has prepared so many avenues to restore our health, He will provide the spiritual elixir to restore the Restoration to its pristine glory as He makes ready a people to labor together to complete the Marvelous Work and a Wonder.

*He prepared a way that they might be healed.*[9]

---

6    Joseph Smith III, *The Saints' Herald*, February 10, 1897.
7    Alma 21:75–76 [46:40].
8    Malachi 4:2.
9    1 Nephi 5:144 [17:41].

# 5

# Our Genetic Pool

*And he said unto me, Behold, there are save two churches only:*
*The one is the church of the Lamb of God, and the other is the*
*church of the devil.*[1]

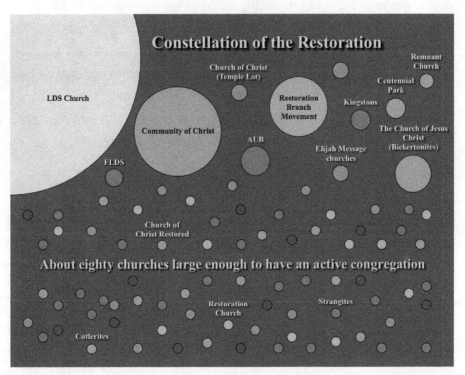

**Constellation of the Restoration**

LDS Church

Church of Christ
(Temple Lot)

Remnant
Church

Centennial
Park

Community of Christ

Restoration
Branch
Movement

Kingstons

The Church of Jesus
Christ
(Bickertonites)

FLDS

AUB

Elijah Message
churches

Church of
Christ Restored

About eighty churches large enough to have an active congregation

Restoration
Church

Strangites

Cutlerites

Scientists tell us that a population with more genetic variation has a better chance of surviving and flourishing than a population with limited genetic differences. Their research affirms that hereditary diversity decreases the occurrence of the unfavorable congenital traits. Some of the individuals in the group can hold traits that make them resistant to such factors as disease or tolerance to the heat or cold, increasing the group's chance for survival when these individuals breed with the others. Conversely, in small isolated populations, individuals may be forced to breed with close relatives, increasing the occurrence

1    1 Nephi 3:220–221 [14:10].

of genetic flaws. When inbreeding occurs, innate weaknesses found in the parents can be multiplied into future generations.

Within the Restoration there are both historical and spiritual variations among the Saints. All branches of the Restoration have typically viewed this as problematic, having stood aloof in an attempt to keep their spiritual gene pools untainted or free of contamination, that they might remain pristine. However, by isolating our spiritual gene pools, we have limited our ability to fight off the disease of criticism and unbelief surrounding the Saints. There are numerous casualties in the spiritual war in which we are all engaged, and many have become lost to the work, regardless of which portion of the Restoration they hail from. In our divided condition we have not yet redeemed Zion, gathered Israel, or witnessed the fall of Babylon. The honest in heart among the children of men are still waiting for the divine expression of the sons of God.

Within the plant and animal kingdoms, more genetic variability leads to the likelihood that their offspring will be resistant to disease and will survive. The same is true in the spiritual life of the church. This type of spiritual genetic diversity can result in an offspring with unique genetic blueprints—different from either parent or, in this case, our various church organizations. The Book of Mormon reminds us that God has been in the process of joining different groups of people to keep them viable in previous generations:

*Now, if we had not grafted in these branches, the tree thereof would have perished.[2]*

The prophetic Book of Mormon foretells of our day and promises to help strengthen and preserve the spiritual gene pool of His ancient covenant people, the house of Israel:

*And the branches of the natural tree will I graft in again, into the natural tree; and the branches of the natural tree will I graft into the natural branches of the tree; and thus will I bring them together again, that they*

2    Jacob 3:56 [5:18].

*shall bring forth the natural fruit; and they shall be one.*[3]

This allegory pertaining to the diaspora of Israel and their eventual gathering is also applicable to the Scattered of the Restoration. Remember, Nephi taught us that we can *"liken all scriptures unto us that it might be for our profit and learning."*[4] In our day the God of Israel will accomplish in the Restoration Movement what He purposes to do with the whole house of Israel—splicing His Saints together to become resistant to the maladies of censure, reproach, and unbelief by our opponents—to create a spiritually strong and healthy people who will bear His image as realized in Zion's redemption.

---

*Having made known unto us the mystery of his will, according to his good pleasure which he hath purposed in himself; that in the dispensation of the fullness of times he might gather together in one all things in Christ, both which are in heaven, and which are on earth; even in him.*[5]

§

### The Ministry of Angels

*And of the angels he saith, Angels are ministering spirits … sent forth to minister for them who shall be heirs of salvation.*[6]

### Sister Marie McGuire
### The Church of Jesus Christ (Bickertonite)

In 1950, I was living in Cape Girardeau, Missouri, with my in-laws. My husband Harry was serving in the U.S. Navy, stationed in Chicago, Illinois, waiting for orders to ship overseas. At this time my in-laws were unacquainted with any of our church people, and I told them very little about our church.

---

3    Jacob 3:133 [5:67].
4    1 Nephi 6:5 [19:23].
5    Ephesians 1:9–10.
6    Hebrews 1:7, 14.

33

While I was living at my in-laws, my son Michael (we call him Mickey today) was born on Wednesday, September 27, 1950. After Mickey was born, while still in the hospital, I was unaware that there was anything wrong with my child. He appeared to me to be a healthy tiny baby. On the last day before we were discharged from the hospital, the doctor who delivered Mickey came into the room to talk to me. He told me that the baby was born with a knot behind his left ear, and at this time it was a little larger than the size of a pea, and it would grow very rapidly. Naturally, as any mother and this being my first child, I was very upset and very frightened. This was Monday, October 2. My mother-in-law picked Mickey and me up from the hospital and took us home.

I noticed the knot had gotten larger, to about the size of a nickel. On Friday October 6, late in the afternoon, nine days after Mickey was born, the doctor came to the house to see how my baby was doing. By that time, the mass had grown to the size of a quarter. The doctor told me that surgery was needed to remove this mass, and it was imperative that I give him an answer. I became more upset and could not bear the thought of having a little baby undergo surgery. My heart was very heavy at this time. I had been praying all along, and I felt my prayers were not being answered. My mother-in-law and father-in-law tried to console me the best they could. We were in touch with the naval authorities, and my husband was unable to be granted a leave of absence as he already had his orders to ship out to Hawaii. I felt so alone, and I felt that the Lord had forsaken me. I had nowhere to go, no one to turn to. My family, the brothers, the sisters, and the church were far away from me; I felt I was deserted. I also felt the Lord was not hearing my prayers, and Mickey was suffering.

Suddenly a thought came to me—that I must call my mother living in New Jersey at the time. I told the doctor that I had to put my decision aside a few more days, and I could not give him an answer that day. The doctor told me I was taking an awful chance and that maybe I wouldn't have Mickey that long. I replied to him that whatever would happen, would be the Lord's will. I had something I must do first. He shrugged his shoulders as if puzzled and left. After he left the house, I told my mother-in-law that I needed to call my mother in New Jersey to have a baby garment blessed for Mickey by the elders of our church. I know she didn't understand and didn't know what I was talking about. I told her I would explain everything to her later.

I called my mother, briefly explaining to her what the doctor said about the baby. I asked her if she would purchase an undershirt, have it blessed by the elders of the church, and send it special delivery as soon as possible. She told me she would. Little did I know at this time what the Lord had in store for us. I went into prayer again, pleading to the Lord to spare my son, but saying, "Thy will, Lord, be done."

On Sunday morning, October 8, around 6:00 a.m. my mother-in-law and I were in the kitchen. She was making a batch of biscuits, and I was sitting at the table drinking a cup of coffee. My father-in-law had gone into town to pick up the Sunday paper, which he usually did. About 6:30 a.m. the doorbell rang. The curtains were still drawn at the kitchen windows, so we couldn't see out. We thought it was probably Dad. Mom went to the door and opened it, and there stood a mailman in the driveway next to his truck. He asked for Mrs. Marie McGuire and said that he had a package for her. I went to the door, and he asked me if I was Marie McGuire. I said yes. He handed me a clipboard and told me to sign by the X mark. He said had a special delivery package, for me, which was tucked under his arm. He handed me the package and I thanked him. He then said good-bye. We watched him get in the mail truck and back out of the driveway. When he reached the end of the driveway, the truck seemed to disappear. We looked to the right and to the left and couldn't see any truck on the road.

I anxiously opened the package to see what was in it. My mother-in-law was standing right by me. After I got the package opened, we saw that it was a baby's undershirt. My eyes quickly swelled up with tears. I looked up at my mother-in-law without exchanging any words. We both went into the bedroom, where the baby was asleep in his crib. I walked over to the crib, and softly and quietly I woke Mickey up. I quickly removed his nightgown and his undershirt. We both looked at the baby's head. The knot behind his ear had grown to the size of a half dollar. I took the new undershirt and proceeded to slip it over Mickey's head. As it passed over the ear, the large mass disappeared before our eyes. At that moment I could not contain myself. I began to sob uncontrollably for there was much joy in my heart at this time, and I could not thank the Lord enough for what He had done for my son. I looked at my mother-in-law, and her face was also tear stained.

I laid my son down in his crib and went quickly to the telephone to call my mom and to thank her for sending the undershirt. As I was talking to her and telling her the beautiful miracle that the Lord just performed on my baby, she told me that she hadn't sent the undershirt yet. She still had it at the house and couldn't get it in the mail until the next day. I then related to her what had taken place that beautiful Sunday morning. We both knew then that the man who just minutes before had stood at the door appearing to be a mailman was not a mailman, but was sent by the Lord as His messenger to deliver a baby garment to spare my son.[7]

> God moves in a mysterious way, His wonders to perform;
> He plants His footsteps in the sea, and rides upon the storm.
> Deep in unfathomable mines of never failing skill,
> He treasures up His bright designs, and works His sovereign will.[8]

## Brother Neil Simmons
## The Reorganized Church of Jesus Christ of Latter Day Saints

The Restoration Movement is rooted in the visitation of heavenly messengers to a young boy named Joseph Smith, Jr. Their testimony to him and to others brought forth the latter-day work with the gospel of the kingdom. Central to the unique doctrinal message of

---

7    Personal correspondence with the author.
8    "God Moves in a Mysterious Way," by William Cowper, penned in 1774.
     William Cowper was a British poet and hymnist.

36

the Restoration is the ministry of angels or the messengers of God. The dictionary defines an angel as a messenger of God or a divine or heavenly messenger. However, many people in our time have doubts about the existence of angels or divine messengers. We note that the letter to the Hebrews in the Bible does give counsel about the presence of angels. They can be in our midst, but they may be unnoticed by the majority of people.

*Be not forgetful to entertain strangers; for thereby some have entertained angels unawares.*[9]

When I was returning from a teaching job in Recife, Brazil, with my younger brother, my wife, and my two very small children, we boarded an ancient creaky DC-4 airplane and headed south to São Paulo, where we hoped we would make flight connections to return to the USA.

I had been enthusiastic about my assignment as an exchange teacher from the Pasadena, California, school system to teach for a year in Brazil. Now that the year was over, we were headed home. I was pleased about our year's experience. We had learned a bit of Portuguese, and our family had spent a restful time at the tropical seashore. We were leaving our house in Recife, south of the equator, and flying much farther south in June, the coldest month of the year in Brazil.

Gathering up all of my travel documents, including money (all cash), passports, and plane tickets for the entire family, I had placed them in a wallet that fit in the inside pocket of the only warm coat that I owned. Trying to manage all the needs of the family on the trip back home was daunting at best, and nearly impossible at times. My son, who was only three years old, felt the need to run everywhere as soon as he got out of the plane and into the terminal. But there was an immense number of people in the airport terminal. They physically pushed and pressed against all of us, threatening to separate my family, by trying to get to their various destinations.

---

9    Hebrews 13:2.

In some desperation I moved our family to the far end of the huge São Paulo terminal and found a spot against the wall well away from the crowds. There they could stand together and wait for me to make a phone call to arrange for a place to stay until our next flight, which was later in the week. Seeing that they were safe and telling my wife and brother to stay right where they were standing so I could find them again out of the masses of people, I walked to the other end of the huge facility, through the multitude of people, to find a telephone.

In those days the money in Brazil was almost valueless. Telephones did not take coins. Instead, we stood in a long line to pay for the use of the phone. After paying several thousand *cruzeiros* (Brazilian dollars) for the use of the phone, I got a number on a slip of paper. Then I stood in another long line outside the phone booth until I was able to enter. I lifted the receiver and read the number to the operator. She agreed that I had paid for the call so she then placed the call for me.

In all that stress and commotion, I had not dared to take the phone number out of my wallet in the line as I waited, fearing I might drop something or that someone might grab it out of my hand and disappear into the mob of people. However, once inside the booth, I took out the wallet. I laid it open upon the small shelf under the phone and extracted the phone number. I gave the number to the operator, who made the call for me. It was successful. I was elated. I hurried out of the phone booth and began pushing my way back through the crowd to find my family and tell them that a car was coming to pick us up and take us where we could get food and spend the night. They were waiting expectantly right where I had left them. As I got near them, the crowd thinned.

Judy, my wife, called out to me, asking if I had been successful. I shouted back, "Yes, I made the call," while at the same time slapping my hand against the outside of my coat to indicate that the phone number in my wallet had worked. As I touched the coat, a terrible realization came upon me. The wallet was not there. I had left it on the small shelf in the phone booth where I had opened it to find the phone number.

As the immensity of that mistake hit my mind, I realized that the wallet was, without a doubt, gone. I had lost all the tickets, passports, and more than $5,000 US dollars. Even so, I whirled about and started to run back to the phone booth more than 1,000 feet away from me and through an immense crowd of people. Just as I turned, I saw directly in front of me, a pleasant looking mature man with a warm smile and seemingly happily amused. He extended toward me my wallet. He was standing alone. There was no other person within 40 or 50 feet of where we both stood except my family still pressed against the wall behind me.

"Neil," he said, "I believe these are yours."

I looked. I took the wallet from his extended hand, checked quickly to see if the tickets, passports, and money were still there. It was intact. I looked up to thank him, but no one was there. In the time it took to flip open the wallet and see all the contents were still there, he was gone. In that moment he could not have gotten back into the masses of people to disappear in the crowd. Instantly, a wonderful sense of the Holy Spirit fell upon me, bringing tears to my eyes and chill bumps on my body as I was prompted to remember the scripture in Hebrews about entertaining angels unawares.

We have treasured that experience in our family for many years, and we believe that one of the three disciples of the Nephite nation was sent to rescue me from utter disaster and my own carelessness. Certainly the blessing that came in that moment was heaven sent. Without it we would have lost everything. Angelic ministry continues to be experienced in the Restoration. I believe that angels still minister to the needs of families who are working to bring to others the message of the gospel of the kingdom.[10]

---

10    Personal correspondence with the author.

## Jammie Townsend
## The Remnant Church of Jesus Christ of Latter Day Saints

When our children were young, my husband, Wesley, worked the night shift and did not get home until after midnight. We lived in a long ranch-style home. The back door was at one end of the house, and our bedroom was at the other end across from our two daughters' bedroom. I always slept with one eye open until Wesley came home for fear that someone might break into the house. We kept a night light on and the doors were locked; but the concern remained.

I tried to stay awake one night while waiting for Wesley, but I kept nodding off. Then a loud noise woke me. My first reaction was to panic. It was too early for Wesley to be home. I lay there praying and wondering what to do next. Then suddenly a personage appeared to me in the doorway of my room. He was dressed in a robe that covered his head, tied at the waist and reached to his feet.

My fears were calmed when I heard the words he reassuringly said to me. "Go back to sleep; I am watching over you." And then he was gone. But I knew I was being watched over.

I know the Lord sends messengers to watch over us and to reassure us in times of distress. Just put your trust in Him.[11]

---

*The Lord of the vineyard said again unto his servant, Look hither, and behold another branch also, which I have planted; behold that I have nourished it also, and it hath brought forth fruit.*[12]

---

11  *Moments with the Master*, Daily Devotional, No. 6, December 11, 2017, The Remnant Church of Jesus Christ of Latter Day Saints.
12  Jacob 3:67, [5:24].

# 6

# An Alternative Plan

*And I saw heaven opened, and behold a white horse; and he that sat upon him is called Faithful and True, and in righteousness he doth judge and make war.*[1]

There once was a moose that wanted to be a horse. The moose had seen a herd of horses, thought they were such elegant and graceful creatures, and wanted to be like them. So he taught himself to be a horse. However, he was never accepted as a horse because, after all, he was really just a moose.

Though many horse owners may simply breed a family mare to a local stallion in order to produce a companion animal, most professional breeders use selective breeding to produce horses of a given phenotype

---
1    Revelation 19:11.

or variety. A horse is generally bred where it is foaled or born. Some breeds denote the country or state where conception took place as the origin of the foal. As these fillies and colts grow the breeder is most concerned about the animal's development through the right nutritional environment. The tissues and organs are all turning over at a great rate, revealing that it is during this time in a horse's life that those feeding the horses can probably have the greatest impact on the future health and athletic performance of these amazing creatures.

Figuratively speaking, within the stables of the Restoration we all believe we are horses, and not moose. Perhaps some even see themselves or at least their particular organization as spirited steeds, foaled in the one true barn, having been given the proper nutrition to ensure development free from contamination, disease, and apostasy!

Alternatively, a breeder could, using horses of differing phenotypes, create a new breed with specific characteristics. Our divine destiny as Saints presupposes that the Master Breeder will use just such an alternative-breeding plan for us. This alternative plan really does foreshadow our future, when we will all be ridden by the Master Equestrian into battle and eventually off into the sunset of the peaceful reign. We share so many, many things in common as inheritors of the everlasting gospel. Can we look out from our stables toward our spiritual fate, with eyes of faith and earnestness to the dawning of a new day? It will be a day when the phenotypes, those spiritually visible characteristics from the various portions of the Restoration, may be bred or combined together to produce the thoroughbreds necessary to run the race to Zion's borderline.

---

*And the armies, which were in heaven, followed him upon white horses,
clothed in fine linen, white and clean.* [2]

---

2    Revelation 19:14.

# Mormon Missionaries Deliver the Fullness of the Gospel[3]

*But behold, it shall come to pass that the Lord God shall say unto him to whom he shall deliver the book, Take these words which are not sealed, and deliver them to another, that he may shew them unto the learned, saying, Read this, I pray thee.*[4]

## Testimony of Brother Stephen Kyriakako
## The Church of Jesus Christ (Bickertonite)

On January 29, 2012, I went out to my car to go to work. I noticed the driver's side door was open and several items were stolen. Among the missing items was my grandfather Rudy Meo's leather case with his Bible and Book of Mormon inside.

This devastated me because he had just passed away a year earlier. For a week, I was torn up at the loss of these books because they were about the only things given to me that belonged to him—and they were just gone.

A week passed, and I was at the monthly fast and prayer meeting at my branch in Irvine, California. As I was still hurt over the incident, they added my name to the prayer list. Brother Paul V. offered the most beautiful prayer that the Lord would return these books to me. I admit I honestly didn't expect what happened next.

After the prayer service—the same day—I got a text from Sister Brenda D., a member of my branch. Her phone number had been in my grandfather's Bible for some time with no name on it, just her phone number. She told me she had received a phone call from some Mormon missionaries regarding a Bible and Book of Mormon they found in the gutter a few days earlier. When the missionaries told her that the name Rudy Meo was on both books, she knew immediately that they belonged to me. Sister Brenda gave me the missionaries' phone number, and I called them.

---

3     D&C 26:2a [27:5].
4     2 Nephi 11:136 [27:15].

Within one hour, I had my grandfather's books back. And not a single piece of paper was missing even though they had spent many days and nights in a gutter. After I was reunited with the books, I looked them over in pure amazement.

Then fear came over me because of how fast this prayer was answered. If there was ever any doubt of a prayer being answered by the Lord after this event, it was completely gone! I give all honor and glory to God for having mercy on me and giving my grandfather's books back to me.[5]

***

## Commentary

How noteworthy it is that at one time the Church of Jesus Christ went to the LDS Church to purchase their Books of Mormon. That favor has been returned as representatives from the LDS Church delivered the lost Scriptures to the rightful owner in The Church of Jesus Christ (Bickertonite). The role of the LDS missionaries in the returned Book of Mormon is, of course, a fine gesture on their part, demonstrating their concern for fellow believers in the book and those Saints to whom it belongs. However, there is more. The warp and woof of our story is a significant stitch in the fabric of the Restored gospel, signaling the prophetic promise of a full circle to reunite all true believers in the angel message.

Let us storm the gates of heaven, asking God to reunite the Saints— removing the obstacles that offend, that we may stand side by side when He makes bare His arm to complete the latter-day evangel.

***

*For the Lord hath heard thy prayers.*[6]

5    "The Miracle of the Stolen Books," The Church of Jesus Christ, Gospel Blog, Monday, July 27, 2015.
6    Mosiah 1:96 [3:4].

# 7

# Cracked Open

*And the time cometh speedily, that the righteous must be led up as calves of the stall, and the Holy One of Israel must reign in dominion, and might, and power, and great glory.*[1]

A geode is a small cavity within a rock lined with crystals or other minerals. From the outside most geodes look like common rocks; but when they are cracked open, the sight can be breathtaking, exhibiting stunning beauty.

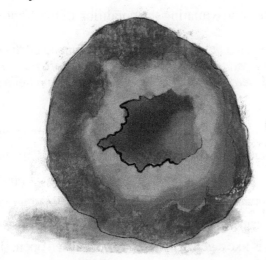

In many ways, geodes are a good representation of the Saints in the Restoration churches. On the exterior we may not always appear to be very attractive, like the larger and more prosperous Catholic and Protestant Churches. Just like a geode, our churches from the outside look common and hardly noticeable; but once the outer shell is penetrated, the elegance of the angel message is marvelously displayed. We testify that the Holy Spirit has been breathed upon His Saints, exhibiting the doctrine, gifts, fruits, and covenants of the Lord. Once we placed our

---

1    1 Nephi 7:55 [22:24].

trust in Jesus and obeyed the everlasting gospel, the Holy Spirit has taken up residence, crystallizing within the Saints the attributes of our Savior. Placed within each of us is the glory of God. However, in our scattered condition the greater exhibition of that glory is often times muted, and the world can't really see it. That shining, shimmering, and radiant countenance is always there, but it has become obscured by the accumulated dust of our history. The full wonder of the Restoration geode is really about an experience that can only occur among a people who are of one accord and in a holy place.[2]

Our story is not only a story about transformation—about becoming different from what we already are—but also about revelation, about the revealing power of a covenant people. Our true identity is as a united and gathered people approximating the condition of the Nephites of old:

> *And surely there could not be a happier people among all the people who had been created by the hand of God. There were no ... manner of ites; but they were in one, the children of Christ, and heirs to the kingdom of God* [3]

May we, the Scattered of the Restoration, begin looking together beneath the accumulated layers of dust that cloud our vision and obscure the precious crystals of the Restored Church. May we look, also, for opportunities to crack open those apparently boring exteriors of our separate churches to reveal more of the beauty that dwells within. The truth of this story is that His glorious church is like a geode, waiting to be cracked open, shimmering and shining with the light, love, and power of the angel message. The early Saints knew that God had called forth His church out of the wilderness, that Zion might arise and put on her beautiful garments.

So, my fellow "theo–geologists," prepare to be amazed by the beauty we will discover when God bends the heavens and shakes the earth to crack wide open the Church, unveiling its celestial splendor, to attract all His Saints and His covenant people scattered upon all the earth.

---

2    Acts 2:1.
3    4 Nephi 1:19 [1:16].

*And it came to pass that I, Nephi, beheld the power of the Lamb of God, that it descended upon the saints of the church of the Lamb, and upon the covenant people of the Lord, who were scattered upon all the face of the earth.[4]*

§

## Called of God by the Gift of Tongues

*God is faithful, by whom ye were called unto the fellowship of his Son Jesus Christ our Lord.[5]*

### Sister Becky Tarbuk
### The Church of Jesus Christ (Bickertonite)

I was raised in the church. It was a wonderful life, and we saw and heard many wonderful things. My earliest memories were going to Sunday school and church several times per week. Sunday dinners were a treat, and it seemed as though everyone was invited. The brothers and sisters would gather around the table rejoicing, happy to be together, with much talk of God's blessings. Discussing the Scriptures, sharing testimonies, and singing were all commonplace. As a child, I always knew that one day I would be baptized and serve God just like my parents, grandparents, and great-grandparents, in the Church of Jesus Christ.

When I became a teen, driving and working, I began to run around with worldly friends, going where they went and doing what they did. But in the back of my mind I always worried that if I died unprepared to meet God, I would be separated from Him. One day I decided that I would begin to pray more and start attending the Sunday and Wednesday evening meetings again (Sunday mornings were a given). I testify that as soon as my heart and mind turned to God, He responded to me.

---

4    1 Nephi 3:230 [14:14].
5    1 Corinthians 1:9.

Shortly thereafter in a Sunday evening service, the elders were closing the meeting and called a brother forward to pray. He said, "Before I pray, I feel to tell the story of blind Bartimaeus. If he hadn't cried out when he did, '*Jesus, thou Son of David, have mercy on me*,'[6] Jesus would never have passed by Bartimaeus again, because He was on his way to the cross."

He concluded and began to pray. As he prayed, he began to speak in tongues with eyes closed and arm extended toward a man who had been attending the church for years and had never asked for his baptism. As a teen in the back of the church watching this, I thought to myself, "Uh-oh Clare, this is your last shot."

Immediately the man praying extended his arm to me and began to speak the Word of the Lord: "Becky, I love you, I love you, I love you. If you will come to Me at this time, I will bless you. If not, you may never be called again." I felt that God knew my heart, and I accepted the call. I asked for my baptism that night at the age of eighteen and have endeavored to be faithful ever since.

I will add that at times I would hesitate to tell my testimony because of the words that were spoken. A few years later, my husband and I were visiting his family in Texas and made an effort to look up the church there. We arrived, and it was just a little modest white square of a building. The windows were open, and the congregation was singing. My mother always said that the gospel had a sound, but that was the first time I had experienced it on my own. They sounded like our people. I could feel the warmth of God's Spirit before we entered the building. The flock was small, and they were all new to me.

Brother Doug M. conducted the Sunday school; and during the lesson, he began to tell his testimony. At the age of thirteen, he was attending a General Church Conference and stood to testify. When he did, there was a brother there who had the gift of singing in the Spirit. His name was Brother Thurman Furiner. He arose and said, "Doug, I love you, I love you,

6    Mark 10:47.

48

I love you" and then Doug asked for his baptism. I was so amazed! What a blessing I felt as he so humbly told his testimony that day.

And so I say, "God loves the whole world, and we were all called to follow Him when Jesus died on Calvary. I am thankful for God's love to me, and the gift of salvation.[7]

## Brother Oscar Case
### The Reorganized Church of Jesus Christ of Latter Day Saints

*As they ministered to the Lord, and fasted, the Holy Ghost said, Separate me Barnabas and Saul for the work whereunto I have called them.[8]*

When I was seventeen years old, I went with my brother to the Western Iowa Reunion of the church, which was held that year, 1889, at Garner's Grove. In every sermon I heard, I was moved by the Spirit of God; and I told my brother Hubert I was going to be baptized as soon as I got home. He said he was, too. So on October 17, 1889, we were both baptized in the River Jordan, a small stream in western Iowa. A wonderful testimony was given to me on that day. Sunday afternoon I went out in the woods to pray. While I was engaged in prayer, a voice spoke to me, telling me the church with which I had united was His; and if I would prepare, I would be permitted to do a good work.

In 1893 my father said to me, "When are you going to take up the ministry?"

I remarked, "God knows my name and address; and if He wants me, He will tell me."

I was teaching school. Another of those western reunions was coming on, and I decided to go. It was to be held at Logan, Iowa, 25 miles from our home. I told Mother I was going.

---

7    Personal correspondence with the author.
8    Acts 13:2.

She said, "What will you do about your school?"

I remarked I'd go down Friday night and come back Sunday night. When I was ready to start from the schoolhouse, I decided to pray about what my Father had asked me. He had told me at that time that he had received a testimony when I was a baby that I would preach the gospel. So I went up there to the desk where I had been teaching all day. I told the Lord all about it and told Him that if He wanted me to preach this gospel, I would like to have Him reveal it to me by moving someone whom I did not know—and in the gift of tongues and interpretation, he would tell me it was in answer to this prayer.

I arrived at the reunion grounds about midnight. A policeman met me and helped me care for my horse and find my tent. There were about 425 tents on the ground. The next morning, I told Hubert I was going to the prayer service. We went together and entered the big tent. There were about 1,500 in that meeting. We went down to about the center.

The meeting had progressed about 15 or 20 minutes. An old gray-haired man, A. H. Rudd, arose directly back of us in the next row of seats. He spoke in an unknown tongue. In the message, he laid his hand on my head at the same time. In the interpretation he said to me:

"Yes, you are called to the ministry, and this is in answer to your prayer you offered at the schoolhouse last evening. You will go to the east, west, north, and south and will be instrumental in baptizing hundreds into the church."[9]

---

*And it came to pass that the Lord of the vineyard said again unto his servant, Look hither, and behold **another branch also**, which I have planted; **behold that I have nourished it also, and it hath brought forth fruit**.*[10]

---

9    *My Book of Acts*, Oscar Case, pp 9–10, Second Edition, Lambert and Moon, Independence, Missouri, 1961.
10   Jacob 3:67, [5:24] emphasis added.

50

# 8

# A Hot-Air Balloon

*For the time cometh, saith the Lamb of God, that I will work a great and a marvelous work among the children of men.*[1]

Four teenagers, three boys and a girl, were out strolling along on a summer day with no particular place to go. Suddenly, there came blowing towards them a piece of paper. They stopped out of curiosity, picked up the paper, and began reading it. It was instructions on "How to Build a Hot Air-Balloon in Four Easy Steps," from the Ensign Balloon Corporation. As they read over the directions, they became more and more excited. "Wow, think of it—to float wonderfully up through the air right up into the clouds—what fun, what excitement!" They resolved at once to build the balloon as quickly as possible before summer ended. They each ran home in great excitement to tell their parents.

The first boy found his dad sitting in the front yard under the big oak

1    1 Nephi 3:214 [14:7].

tree, trying to stay cool. Almost out of breath, he blurted out, "Dad, we found the plans to build a hot-air balloon, and we're going to build one!"

The father slowly fanned himself, cleared his throat, and began speaking: "Son, I know all about such things. First of all, it couldn't work; uh, it never has before. And besides, right in this town we have two fine helium and hydrogen balloon companies, the Luther Balloon Works and the Wesley Balloon Company. Why not simply save your money and go buy one from them? Yes, that is the answer."

The second boy ran home and found his dad sleeping in an easy chair. "Dad, wake up," he said. "We have found the plans to build a hot-air balloon in just four easy steps—all we have to do is ..."

"Wait a minute," the father interrupted. "Four easy steps? Nothing can be done in four easy steps. I'll call my friends together, and we'll appoint a few commissions to study the weather conditions, a commission ..." and his voice trailed off as he headed for the phone.

The third boy found his mother sitting in the living room reading a magazine. "Mom, Mom," he said, "we've found the plans on how to build a hot-air balloon, and we are going to do it."

The mother quickly rose from her chair and said to her son, "Ballooning is dangerous! I'm advising you against this idea, but I'll tell you what we'll do. There is a fine balloonology school called San Paulo's right here in town.[2] Your father and I will send you there to learn more about it."

The young lady raced home to find her father watching TV. She rushed over, placed herself between her dad and the TV and said, "Dad, wait till you hear—we've just found the plans on how to build a hot-air balloon, and we're going to start on it right away."

---

2   The RLDS Church sent its appointee ministers to St. Paul's School of Theology in Kansas City, Missouri, ignoring the counsel given to the elders in the early days of the Restoration: *"Ye are not sent forth to be taught, but to teach the children of men the things which I have put into your hands by the power of my Spirit; and ye are to be taught from on high."* D&C 43:4b–c [43:15–16, BofC 45:15].

The father arose and said, "Honey—sit down for a minute. I've got sad news for you. Everyone knows that hot-air balloons are an archaic concept. They were popular in the 1830s but are no longer in vogue. Seems people really didn't understand it or want it. Too bad," he said as he turned his attention once again to the TV.

Children are kind of impetuous and idealistic. Didn't some great teacher say something once about how we should be like children? Well, undaunted, the four of them met the next day and got right to work. Before long, they had it built. They put their initials on it: Z for Zeke, I for Inez, O for Ollie, and N for Nick, naming it ZION. On a clear day it can be seen floating—floating wonderfully over Independence, Missouri.

---

*And blessed are they who shall seek to bring forth my Zion at that day, for they shall have the gift and the power of the Holy Ghost.*[3]

§

### To Make One Happy

### Testimony of José Almerich
### As told by Jill Stevens
### The Church of Jesus Christ of Latter-day Saints

From 1973–1976 my father, Robert V. Stevens, presided over the LDS mission in Spain. He was accompanied by his wife Sue and their five children. My parents would, as often as possible, take us children with them as they traveled all over Spain to various missionary zone conferences. These were wonderful opportunities for us as children. Often we were overwhelmed by the Spirit and would be strengthened by the talks and powerful testimonies shared in these meetings.

It was no different for my younger brother Matthew. At eight years

---
3    1 Nephi 3:187 [13:37].

of age, Matthew found himself sitting in on the morning session of a Valencia zone conference. Anxious to be like the missionaries, Matthew arrived for the morning session wearing a white shirt and tie. Excited at the lunch break, Matthew begged our mother to let him go outside with some of the missionaries so that he could pass out a Book of Mormon. Reassured by the missionaries that they were happy to watch over my little brother, my mother gave her permission.

Handing Matthew a Book of Mormon in Spanish, my mother asked him, "What do you want to say to someone in Spanish when you give them this book?"

Matthew answered, "Would you like to learn how to be happy?"

And so my mother taught him how to say "*¿Quieres aprender a ser feliz?*"

Matthew replied, "If the gospel makes me happy, then it can make someone else happy, too."

Matthew waited on the street corner that day for over an hour for just the right person to come along to receive his copy of the Book of Mormon. Waiting as patiently as an eight-year-old child possibly could, Matthew soon spotted a twenty-year-old man by the name of José Almerich crossing the street with a letter in his hand. José was headed for a mailbox located on the same street corner where Matthew was standing. Before José could drop his letter into the mailbox, Matthew approached him, handed him the Book of Mormon, and asked him if he wanted to learn to be happy.

Surprised, José told him thank you and took the book home with him. Enclosed was the address of the local meetinghouse, along with the schedules for Sunday services. It was not long afterwards until José showed up at church, having already read the Book of Mormon. He began taking the discussions and in time found that he was ready to be baptized.

On the day of the baptism, José told my father the rest of his story.

José had had a painful childhood. He was sent off to an all-boys boarding school at a very young age, rarely seeing his family for many years to come. Consequently, he received no help, support, or counseling for the physical and emotional abuse he suffered while attending school. Following graduation, he went straight into the armed services. After completing the required two years of military duty, José found himself all alone and extremely lost. Soon he began looking for some kind of meaning or direction to his life. He studied various religions but found no real satisfying answers.

José told my father that—having finally come to the lowest point in his life and having given up all hope for finding family or answers that might help him work through his painful past—he found himself writing a farewell letter to his only friend in the world. He showed the letter to my father and said, "President Stevens, I had no more desire to live. The pain I was suffering was too great, and so I had made the decision to end my life. I wrote my kind friend this letter, asking for his forgiveness, and said my good-byes. On the day I met your Matthew, I was on my way to mail this letter with the plans of returning home quickly to do just that. As I was crossing the street to approach the mail box, I remember physically wiping the tears away from my eyes with the thought that I had never been so unhappy."[4]

---

*And surely there could not be a happier people among all the people who had been created by the hand of God.[5]*

---

4     https://www.plonialmonimormon.com/2017/02/whose-fruit-was-desirable-to-make-one.html

5     4 Nephi 1:19 [1:16].

# 9

# Shake It Off and Step Up

*I give unto men weakness, that they may be humble; and my grace is sufficient for all men that humble themselves before me; for if they humble themselves before me, and have faith in me, then will I make weak things become strong unto them.*[1]

There is a parable about an old mule. The mule fell into a deep dry well and began to cry loudly. Hearing his mule bray, the farmer came over and evaluated the situation. The well was deep, and the mule was heavy. He knew it would be difficult, if not impossible, to lift the animal out. Because the mule was old and the well was dry, the farmer decided to bury the animal in the well. In this way he could solve two problems: put the old mule out of his misery and have his well filled.

1    Ether 5:28 [12:27]

The farmer called upon his neighbors to assist him, and they agreed to help. To work they went. Shovelful of dirt after shovelful of dirt began to fall on the mule's back. The old mule became hysterical. Then all of a sudden an idea came to the mule. Each time they would throw a shovelful of dirt on his back, he could shake it off and step up. Shovelful after shovelful, the mule would shake it off and step up, shake it off and step up. Pretty soon, the old mule stepped up over the edge of the well and trotted off, to the shock and astonishment of all the neighbors. That, which could have buried him, actually blessed him—all due to the manner in which he handled his adversity.

Could the old mule represent the Restoration, and the farmer and his neighbors be the churches of the world which have combined against the Saints and the covenant people of the Lord to bury the Book of Mormon and the truth of God's Word? There are many people who don't realize or have forgotten that the Book of Mormon is in fact, a book and not just a hit musical. Today it is not merely socially acceptable to mock and dismiss the book, but it is prerequisite for being taken seriously by those who dismiss the angel message.[2]

Following the death of Joseph Smith, Jr., the church fractured, making it difficult to speak with one voice to declare the everlasting gospel to a world darkened in sin. Perhaps in the wisdom of the Lord who presides over the destinies of men and kingdoms, there has been a purpose all along, hiding Virtue away in the midst of many contesting factions, where she has remained until this day—her worth yet unknown, her praises unsung, until He makes bare His arm to reveal her majesty.

For Book of Mormon believers, the assaults on the latter-day work can in reality be used to lift us up out of the well of opposition so we can step into the Holy City, gather Israel, and stand in holy places. As we watch for the return of our Savior, may the Scattered of the Restoration, shake off our differences and step up, becoming malleable in His hands!

---

2    Avi Steinberg, *The Lost Book of Mormon, A Quest for the Book That Just Might Be the Great American Novel*, p. 10, www.penguinrandomhouse.com/books.

*Shake off the chains with which ye are bound, and come forth out of*
*obscurity, and arise from the dust.*[3]

§

## God Shall Remove the Obstacles

*Is any sick among you? Let him call for the elders of the church; and let*
*them pray over him, anointing him with oil in the name of the Lord; and*
*the prayer of faith shall save the sick, and the Lord shall raise him up;*
*and if he have committed sins, they shall be forgiven him.*[4]

### Brother Kevin Murphy
### The Church of Jesus Christ (Bickertonite)

On Sunday, February 2, 2014, during our anointing service, we had a
brother using a cane approach the ministry. This brother had been
suffering from knee issues for a very long time. He had been through a
couple surgeries with no relief. Although he had been anointed for this
injury before, he felt he needed to be anointed again.

We circled around him and waited for the Spirit to move upon one of
us. A brother elder stepped forward and started to pray. The prayer was
a call to heal this brother. Once he stated these words, everyone heard a
loud noise.

The prayer ended, and the brother walked away without his cane,
leaving it up front. We then went into the testimony part of our service.
After a few testimonies, the brother with the bad knee stood and
proclaimed that he tried to make his knee hurt with no success. His son
walked up to the front of the sanctuary and picked up his father's cane.
It had broken in half.

The gift of tongues came forth with the interpretation being, "This is
My power, thus saith the Lord." We thank God for His love and mercy.[5]

---

3     2 Nephi 1:39 [1:23].
4     James 5:14–15.
5     The Church of Jesus Christ, The Gospel Blog, February 25, 2014.

# Brother Samuel Twombly
## The Reorganized Church of Jesus Christ of Latter Day Saints

*For, behold, I will bless all those who labor in my vineyard, with a mighty blessing.[6]*

S amuel Twombly was laboring as a missionary in western Nebraska. He held a morning service and planned to ride his bicycle about 20 miles for an afternoon service. But a terrible rainstorm began. It rained and rained. Samuel kept thinking, "Should I go? Should I go?" Finally he decided, "Yes, I will go. It is my responsibility to go there and minister to those people."

Samuel began riding along the railroad track in the pouring rain. Arriving at a river, he saw that the bridge was covered by wildly rushing water. He thought, "There is no way I can fulfill my promise." He knelt in the mud and began praying to God. He said, "Lord, I need to be there, but You saw fit not to provide the means. Would You minister to the people who will be waiting for me?" After praying, he stood and turned to go back home. But he almost walked into the river because he found himself on the opposite side!

Samuel was indeed blessed to accomplish his mission for the Lord. There is power in obeying the commands of God and in working for Him.[7]

---

*And it came to pass that the Lord of the vineyard, and also the servant, went down into the vineyard to labor.[8]*

6    D&C 19:3a, [21:9], BofC 22:10. Received by Joseph Smith, Jr., April 6, 1830.
7    *True Restoration Experiences*, Compiled by Clara Thomas, p. 5, Sionita School, Inc., Bates City, Missouri, 1985.
8    Jacob 3:50 [5:16].

# 10

# Broken Pottery

*But he knoweth the way that I take: when he hath tried me, I shall come forth as gold.[1]*

When a potter makes a bowl, he creates it by hand with soft pliable clay. The bowl is formed to the potter's liking and then fired to about 1,500 degrees. Afterwards, it is finished and presented as a true work of art. If we had a bowl that broke, would we even consider repairing it, especially if it were broken into several different pieces—let alone consider it more beautiful for having been broken? Probably not! If a bowl were to become broken into multiple pieces, it would more than likely be discarded. We, especially in Western civilization, would simply dispose of it by tossing it out in the trash.

But in some cultures, the owner would not only repair it, but also elevate it to a whole new level of appreciation. There is a centuries-old Japanese art of fixing broken pottery called kijtsugi (golden joinery) or

---

1    Job 23:10.

kintsukuroi (golden repair). A special golden lacquer creates beautiful seams of gold to sparkle and shine in the cracks of the ceramic ware, giving a unique appearance to the piece. This repair method accentuates the artifact's unique history by emphasizing the fractures and breaks instead of hiding or disguising them. This method of restoration often makes the piece even more beautiful than the original, revitalizing the artifact with new life.

Of course, we all recognize this simile in the life, ministry, death, and resurrection of our Lord Jesus. The brokenness of our lives can be seen in His sacrifice, and with His scars is made more beautiful to us because *"with his stripes we are healed."*[2]

How might this allegory also apply to the Scattered of the Restoration? We all sprang out of the original Restored Church, which we could identify as our ceramic bowl. Each organization or piece of the bowl has viewed the breaking up of the pottery or the church as the only way to separate itself from the rest of the bowl, which had too many impurities, thus preserving the fragment's integrity by freeing it of contamination and apostasy. However, with the various pieces broken off, no matter how pristine we believe our fragment of the bowl is, unless we are mended, the bowl cannot hold that for which it was designed.

Remember, in the art of kintsukuroi, the master artesian uses a golden lacquer to repair the crack. In the Restoration we, too, have the golden lacquer, the golden Bible—our Book of Mormon. As we rally around this standard, our fractures can be viewed as fortunate, which now will allow the repairing of the bowl—or the healing of the breach—by the Lord Jesus, actually making the Restored Church more beautiful and precious than our individual parts ever have been. The unique gifts and traits formed during our period of separation have matured and developed to such a degree that—when blended with one another—will allow the Body of Christ to remember its unique history and to once again sparkle and shine with the testimony of Jesus, as realized in Zion's redemption.

---

2    Isaiah 53:5, Mosiah 8:20 [14:5].

*And they that shall be of thee shall build the old waste places; thou shalt raise up the foundations of many generations; and thou shalt be called, The repairer of the breach.*[3]

§

## Miraculously Protected

*Wherefore, he will preserve the righteous by his power.*[4]

### Brother Ishmael D'Amico
### The Church of Jesus Christ (Bickertonite)

While I was employed in the construction of a building in Detroit, in November 1921, I was handing material to the bricklayer. I was standing on a board about one foot wide, which was supported by a scaffold, some distance from the ground. Suddenly the board upon which I stood broke and fell to the ground; but I remained standing in mid-air, safe and sound. I was neither injured nor afraid, and I glorified God that I was preserved, although the board had broken and fallen from under me. I then stepped over to other boards, which had not broken. It was just as if someone had held me up until I could reach a place of safety.

Later I was telling this experience in a testimony meeting here in Detroit. The Spirit of God descended on one of the brothers. He saw in a vision that when the board had broken, the Lord Jesus Himself came and held me by my arms to keep me from falling.

I thank our Lord again and again that He saved me from perishing.[5]

---

3    Isaiah 58:12.
4    1 Nephi 7:36 [22:17].
5    *A History of the Church of Jesus Christ* [Bickertonite], Vol. 1, p. 151.

## Brother Earl Phillips
## The Reorganized Church of Jesus Christ of Latter Day Saints

I was approaching a railroad crossing in my big truck. I was thinking about many other things and glanced down the track without paying much attention. I did not see any train, so I started across the tracks. Suddenly looking up, I saw a train right there upon me. I quickly pushed the accelerator to the floor and felt as though the truck leaped across the tracks as the whistling train flew by just behind me.

Very much puzzled, I thought over the experience as I drove on to town. Several times I pushed the accelerator to the floor to see if the truck would leap again as it had across the tracks, but it did not. I did not understand what had happened, so I went to the railroad station where the train had stopped.

The engineer recognized my truck and rushed over to it. I thought, "Now, here is where I am going to get a bawling out."

"Say," the engineer spoke excitedly, "when I saw you back there on that track, I thought there was no possible way of missing you. I started to close my eyes. Then to my amazement I saw a big hand reach down from the heavens, grab your truck, and pull it across the tracks!"

As the engineer spoke, I knew that a divine hand had moved to spare my life.[6]

---

*And they became like unto one body; and the fruit were equal; and the Lord of the vineyard had preserved unto himself the natural fruit, which was most precious unto him from the beginning.*[7]

---

6    *True Restoration Adventures*, Compiled by Clara Thomas, p. 22, Sionita School, Inc., Bates City, Missouri, 1986.
7    Jacob 3:144 [5:74].

64

# 11

# Cohesive Zooids

> The cause of God is one common cause, in which the Saints are alike all interested ... and possess alike the same glorious hope. The advancement of the cause of God and the building up of Zion is as much one man's business as another.[1]

My four-year-old grandson Parker introduced me to a remarkable sea creature. This "creature" is not actually a creature at all, but multiple tiny creatures, called zooids, all living and working together. They combine to create what's called a siphonophore, a long, thin, sometimes transparent floating colony that can cursorily resemble a jellyfish.

This is a newly discovered species that has yet to be fully identified.

1    Quote from Joseph Smith, Jr., *History of the Church* [LDS], Vol. 4, p. 609, Deseret Books, Salt Lake City, Utah, 1949.

The colonial siphonophore is composed of many physiologically cohesive zooids. Each zooid is structurally similar to other independent animals, but the zooids are all attached to each other, rather than living independently. Each zooid is highly specialized. For example, there are nectophores, which propel the colony forward but lack the ability to feed, whereas the feeding polyps allow the creature(s) to eat but not swim. So basically, each individual organism lacks the functionality that another one has, and therefore each relies on its friends to do what it cannot. These zooids are entirely individual creatures working together to form one large creature, allowing the entire colony to function as a single organism. Most zooids are so specialized they lack the ability to survive on their own.

The siphonophore is a great prophetic symbol found in nature, illustrating the divine destiny for the Scattered of the Restoration. Each branch of the church has a particular function to play and is a part of something bigger than itself in the unfolding drama of Zion and her redemption. Typically the Saints view the church as an organization. But God, on the other hand, designed His church to be a living organism, active and breathing the gospel of the kingdom, which is *"righteousness, peace, and joy in the Holy Ghost."* [2] When God moves to heal the breach among us, there will be an unstoppable synergy that becomes the force of the Body of Christ on earth, ushering in the kingdom of God and gathering His scattered children home.

The Saints of the Restoration really have the same common aspiration of Zion, that community of believers who, through their inner connectedness to Christ and His everlasting gospel, are called to become of one heart and one mind. Then, like the siphonophore, we will reveal the glory of God when we function as the single organism He intended His church to be.

---

2    Romans 14:17.

*And thus will I bring them together again, that they shall bring forth the natural fruit; and they shall be one.*[3]

§

## I Heard These Hymns Before

*That which hath been is now; and that which is to be hath already been.*[4]

### Brother Ed Colyer
### The Restoration Branch Movement

L ast Sunday [March 15, 2015] was quite emotional for me. I knew about the Book of Mormon event on Saturday.[5] Then, on Sunday I watched the Zarahemla Ustream event of testimonies.[6] I certainly was paying attention. But, as the sister began to sing the hymn, "Won't It Be Something to See Israel Smile," I began to weep. Something was happening. Then, during her singing of the second song, "Whose Children Are These," I was completely overcome.

I write of this because of the events I experienced as a young lad of maybe two or three years of age. Many years ago, Mom tells me I had a three-day experience while lying on the bed, knees drawn up, and one leg crossed over the other leg. She said all of a sudden I began to carry on a conversation much like an adult—only I could barely talk at the time. After listening to me carry on the conversation or conversations, she began to question me: "Who are you talking to?" "Where are you?" "What kind of a place is it?" On and on my mother would ask me.

And each and every time I would reply; "I am talking to the angels." "It is a pretty place." "I am in heaven." After three days, these conversations ended; and like any very young lad I continued doing what a young boy would do.

---

3    Jacob 3:134, [5:68].
4    Ecclesiastes 3:15.
5    Book of Mormon Event in Zion Conference, March 13–14, 2015.
6    Zarahemlabranch.org

Quite frankly, I seem to have forgotten these conversations for many years. Then one day, just prior to Mom's dying, I began to have times when I would seemingly have what I call a flashback—where I knew and understood events taking place. By this time I was age 71.

Last Sunday, all of a sudden, I recalled the words to the hymns, "Whose Children Are These" and "Won't It Be Something to See Israel Smile." I had heard these before. As a matter of fact, I had sung these hymns before. I had heard and sung them during my young age during those three days while carrying on those conversations. Yet, as soon as the hymns ended, I could not recall one word. Yet, in those few minutes I knew them. I knew those words, I had been there before. I had heard them sung by those angels I was talking with as a wee young lad.[7]

------

# Commentary

I have heard Sister Arlene Buffington relate that as she traveled among the Native American members of The Church of Jesus Christ, sharing and teaching *The Songs of Zion*, several times she heard individuals testify that they, too, had heard these songs before. This could not be true unless these songs had been planted in their memory by the unseen power of the Holy Spirit. Why a remnant of Joseph? Why Brother Colyer? Why now?

There is a stirring, a whispering of the Spirit, that the day we have prayed, dreamed, longed, and hoped for is soon to dawn. The messages breathed into *The Songs of Zion* testifies of our latter-day theme, with the gathering of Israel to the Holy City, to which Jesus will return to make up His jewels. The Holy Spirit continues to be manifest amongst the Scattered of the Restoration, blending us together one note at a time. Sing Glory!

------

7    Personal communication sent to the author.

Gather her babies, all her young men,
All her fair daughters, go gather them in;
Raise from the dust and the tears where they bow;
Won't it be something to see Israel smile![8]

8    Arlene Buffington, *The Songs of Zion,* Vol. 1, No.100, Chorus to "Won't It Be
Something to See Israel Smile."

# 12

# The Iron Axhead

*And the sons of the prophets said unto Elisha, Behold now, the place where we dwell with thee is too strait for us. Let us go, we pray thee, unto Jordan, and take thence every man a beam, and let us make us a place there, where we may dwell. And he answered, Go ye. And one said, Be content, I pray thee, and go with thy servants. And he answered, I will go. So he went with them. And when they came to Jordan, they cut down wood. But as one was felling a beam, the axhead fell into the water; and he cried, and said, Alas, master! For it was borrowed. And the man of God said, Where fell it? And he showed him the place. And he cut down a stick, and cast it in thither; and the iron did swim. Therefore, said he, Take it up to thee. And he put out his hand, and took it.[1]*

Elisha, whose name means "God is salvation," cut down a stick and placed it in the water, and the iron axhead swam to it. John Newton, a former captain of a slave ship and author of the hymn "Amazing Grace," once wrote:

---
1    2 Kings 6:1–7.

Not one concern of ours is small,
If we belong to Him,
To teach us this, the Lord of all,
Once made the iron to swim.[2]

For Book of Mormon believers there is a prophetic significance to this story. Lehi was shown the rod of iron. Nephi desired to see and understand what his father saw. He was then visited by a heavenly messenger and beheld a panoptic vision of the tree of life and was told the meaning of the rod of iron:

*And it came to pass that I beheld that the rod of iron, which my father had seen, was the word of God.[3]*

Later Nephi would declare,

*And now, my beloved brethren, and also Jew, and all ye ends of the earth, hearken unto these words, and believe in Christ; and if ye believe not in these words, believe in Christ. And if ye shall believe in Christ, ye will believe in these words; for they are the words of Christ, and he hath given them unto me; and they teach all men that they should do good.[4]*

The divine commission given to the Restoration is to use this book (Lehi's rod of iron) to complete the Savior's work. Jesus was lifted up and nailed upon a wooden cross so that the children of Israel, who have been scattered and driven, can be attracted to our Lord, His doctrine, and the lands of their inheritance in these last days. Each church of the Restoration possesses this remarkable record. Each of its members claim an authorative baptism, which baptism should cause the Saints to be attracted to this rod of iron, that the Saints and His covenant people might swim to our Savior and rest on Zion's peaceful shores.

---

*Wherefore, the Lord God will proceed to make bare his arm in the eyes of all the nations, in bringing about his covenants and his gospel, unto those who are of the house of Israel.[5]*

2    "The Borrowed Axe," John Newton, *Olney Hymns*, Vol. 1, No. 39, Forgotten Books, 2012.
3    1 Nephi 3:68 [11:25].
4    2 Nephi 15:11–12 [33:10].
5    1 Nephi 7:22 [22:11].

§

## Put Them Together

*But his word was in mine heart as a burning fire shut up in my bones.*[6]

### Brother Robert Gonzales
### The Church of Jesus Christ (Bickertonite)

In 1985 Robert Gonzales was a member of another faith. He was so convinced that the Book of Mormon was a book of the devil, that he had taught classes to this effect. He later found himself living with the Palacios family in Lorain, Ohio, who belonged to the Church of Jesus Christ. Here is his testimony:

While there, I visited the Niles Branch; and they were talking about the Book of Mormon. I had been told about the Book of Mormon and the different things in it, what it's about and everything. But then Sister Rose [Palacios] was telling me about it; and she told me that if I didn't believe her, to take it to God with a "broken heart and contrite spirit," and God would reveal the truth to me.

A few days after that, we again visited the Niles Branch. Sister Rose stood up, and she had the Bible in one hand and the Book of Mormon in the other. She said, "This is the Word of God, just like it says in Ezekiel." Then she put them together up over her head. When she put them together, [I saw] they burst into flames. Then I knew that God was telling me that this was true.[7]

### Testimony of Robert Robinson as told by Patrick S. McKay, Sr.

In 2013 while on a missionary trip to southern California, we contacted an individual named Robert Robinson. He had been briefly associated with a couple of different Restoration churches several years earlier, and was presently attending a Greek Orthodox church. He shared how

---

6    Jeremiah 20:9.
7    http://www.thechurchofjesuschrist.org/blog/item/my-restoration-testimony

happy he was to be worshipping in this setting. However, wanted to also tell us about a marvelous testimony he had received regarding the Book of Mormon. Here is what he shared:

"I dreamed I saw a stream; and in the stream was floating a book, the Bible. Then, coming up out of the water, I saw another book which was the Book of Mormon. I then saw that the two books merged into one book in my hand."

Although Robert Robinson no longer worships in the Restoration, he still believes the Book of Mormon to be scripture and equal with the Bible. We invited Robert to continue to consider the Book of Mormon, to read and study it, to pray about it, and experiment upon the principles woven within its pages.

The Book of Mormon is the *magnum opus* of the Restoration. As Robert Robinson was advised, we, too, should search and ponder this record. Just as the book can and does transform lives, it can and will transform the Scattered of the Restoration by the same Spirit which testifies to us of its truth, uniting us as God moves to deliver the Saints to the Holy Mount of Zion.

------------

*Moreover, thou son of man, take thee one stick and write upon it, for Judah, and for the children of Israel his companions; then take another stick, and write upon it, for Joseph, the stick of Ephraim, and for all the house of Israel his companions; And join them one to another into one stick; and they shall become one in thine hand.*[8]

------------

8    Ezekiel 37:16–17.

# 13

# The Set Time Has Come

*Thou shalt arise, and have mercy upon Zion; for the time to favor her, yea, the set time, is come.*[1]

It was late fall, and the Indians on a remote reservation in Oklahoma asked their new chief if the coming winter was going to be cold or mild. Since he was a chief in a modern society, he had never been taught the old secrets. When he looked at the sky, he couldn't tell what the winter was going to be like. Nevertheless, to be on the safe side, he told his tribe that the winter was indeed going to be cold and that the members of the village should collect firewood to be prepared.

But being a practical leader, after several days, he got an idea. He picked up the phone and called the National Weather Service and asked, "Is the coming winter going to be cold?"

---

1    Psalm 102:13.

The chief was told, "It looks like this winter is going to be quite cold." So the chief went back to his people and told them to collect even more firewood in order to be prepared.

A week later, he called the National Weather Service again, "Does it still look like it's going to be a very cold winter?" he asked.

"Yes," the man at the National Weather Service again replied, "it's going to be a very cold winter." The chief again went back to his people and ordered them to collect every scrap of firewood they could find.

Two weeks later, the chief called the National Weather Service once again. "Are you absolutely sure that the winter is going to be very cold?"

"Absolutely," the man replied. "It's looking more and more like it's going to be one of the coldest winters we've ever seen."

"How can you be so certain?" the chief asked.

The weatherman replied, "The Indians are collecting carloads of firewood!"

Just as we see illustrated in our story, societal influences can lead to the public's acquiescence. Our common testimony of the restoration of the house of Israel and the building of a Holy City longed for by the Scattered of the Restoration yet remains opaque to the society around us. If the Saints could unite and begin collecting firewood, as it were, we could influence the millions yet waiting for the manifestation of the sons of God as they witness the towers of Zion illumine the skyline, while her streets of gold become transparent, reflecting the pure light of God's glory. The Scriptures scream out at us regarding our divine destiny, *"Thou shalt arise, … for the time to favor her, yea the set time, is come."* [2] Therefore, *"Awake, awake, put on thy strength, O Zion; put on thy beautiful garments."* [3]

---

2   Psalm 102:13.
3   2 Nephi 5:112 [17:30].

*And thus will I bring them together again, that they shall bring forth the natural fruit; and they shall be one.*[4]

§

## They Shall Carry Them Forth

*For after the book of which I have spoken shall come forth, and be written unto the Gentiles, and sealed up again unto the Lord, there shall be many which shall believe the words which are written; and they shall carry them forth unto the remnant of our seed.*[5]

### Sister Elsie Hensley
### The Restoration Branch Movement

While Richard and I were living on the Navajo Reservation in Piñón, Arizona, I was involved in teaching classes for the women. I used my Scriptures and had many notes and loose pages tucked inside of them.

At one point, we decided to take a couple of weeks off and travel back to Independence, Missouri, for a visit. I wanted to take my Scriptures with me, so I packed them in my suitcase. After the two-week visit, we made the long trip back to Piñón. We arrived in the evening. When I unpacked my suitcase, I realized to my great dismay that I had left my Scriptures beside the bed where we had been staying in Independence. I was so upset because I could not teach the classes without them. I felt desperate. Richard and I prayed for help before we went to bed. The next morning when I awoke, I looked over at the bedside table. There were my Scriptures stacked neatly on the table.[6]

---

4    Jacob 3:134 [5:68].
5    2 Nephi 12:80 [30:4].
6    *Heritage Series*, No. 107, "They Shall Carry Them Forth," Published by Patrick S. McKay, Sr., Independence, Missouri, December 12, 2015.

# Commentary

In Moroni's Preface to the Book of Mormon, he writes that the primary purpose of this record is to restore the remnants of the house of Israel to a knowledge of the covenants God made with their fathers. He also declared the book was, *"Written to the Lamanites which are a remnant of the house of Israel; and also to Jew and Gentile."* Through revelation Oliver Cowdery was told, *"Thou shalt go unto the Lamanites, and preach my gospel unto them."*[7]

The first mission of the Restored Church was to take this record to the Lamanites. Peter Whitmer, Jr., Parley P. Pratt and Ziba Peterson joined Oliver Cowdery on this errand. They had preached the gospel in its fullness among the Cattaraugus Indians near Buffalo, New York, the Wyandots of Ohio, and the Delawares in Kansas, distributing the record of their forefathers to them. Since that day many have labored from the various branches of the Restored Church, attempting to prosecute the work among descendants of the Book of Mormon peoples. Sister Hensley's testimony is merely one of many evidences that the God of Israel is blessing these attempts.

The day is fast approaching when a coordinated effort will be manifest by a united ministry fulfilling the hopes, desires, and dreams of these early missionaries, as codified in the eloquent and prophetic language of Parley P. Pratt:

> We trust that at some future day, when the servants of God go forth in power to the remnant of Joseph, some precious seed will be found growing in their hearts, which was sown by us in that early day.[8]

---

7   D&C 27:3a [28:8], BofC 30:7.
8   *Autobiography of Parley P. Pratt*, pp. 44–45, Deseret Book Co., Salt Lake City, Utah, 1985.

*And the gospel of Jesus Christ shall be declared among them; wherefore, they shall be restored unto the knowledge of their fathers, and also to the knowledge of Jesus Christ, which was had among their fathers. And then shall they rejoice.*[9]

9    2 Nephi 12:82–83 [30:5–6].

# 14

# Blended Vision

*And I would, my brethren, that ye should know that all the kindreds of the earth cannot be blessed unless he shall make bare his arm in the eyes of the nations.[1]*

As most people age, there is a progressive loss of the ability to see things up close. The lens of the eye gradually loses its flexibility, making it more and more difficult to focus clearly on close objects such as printed words. There is a form of Lasik surgery called blended vision, which can adjust our sight. Blended vision works by increasing the depth of field of each eye through subtle changes in the optics of the cornea. The increase in the depth of field allows for the eyes to be corrected in such a way that the dominant eye is set for distance and intermediate vision while the non-dominant eye sees best in the intermediate to near

1    1 Nephi 7:21 [22:10].

range. In Lasik blended vision, the eyes are effectively working together to allow good vision up close, intermediate, and far away without the use of glasses. The ophthalmologist will operate on the weaker eye, making it slightly short sighted, which will improve close up vision.

As Saints, we share the common view or belief that we all belong to the "one true church." When we become fixated on this a little too hard, we may miss the good things going on around us in other parts of the Restoration—leaving them slightly out of focus. In our zeal and desire to be "right," our hyper-focus mode has distorted our vision. Sometimes we can be recipients of additional blessings if we willingly blur traditional boundaries [not doctrine] that have separated us for too long.

Figuratively speaking, all the Saints could benefit from this type of spiritual Lasik surgery, making our path clearer as God moves to reunite His Saints. Moroni, who saw our day, reminds us:

> I give unto men **weakness**, that they may be humble; and my grace is sufficient for all men that humble themselves before me; for if they humble themselves before me, and have faith in me, then will **I make weak things become strong** unto them.[2]

I am the first to acknowledge there are differences, some significant; but understand, too, that friendships unite! When we consider our divine destiny as Saints of the latter days, our hearts should be made glad as we fellowship collectively. May these genuine friendships allow the Scattered of the Restoration to receive the blessings of blended vision, witnessing the Saints effectively working together as we experience a foretaste of those joys which will be ours when we are finally gathered together into the Holy City.

---

*Wo unto the wise in their own eyes, and prudent in their own sight!* [3]

---

2    Ether 5:28 [12:27] Emphasis added.
3    2 Nephi 8:91 [15:21].

# A Parting of the Veil

*Wherefore, we search the prophets; and we have many revelations,
and the spirit of prophecy, and having all these witnesses, we obtain a
hope, and our faith becometh unshaken.*[4]

## Brother Robert Millet
## The Church of Jesus Christ of Latter-day Saints

Below is a transcription of his testimony, which he shared with the Zarahemla Branch, following the 2015 Book of Mormon Symposium.

My father was raised in the church in Louisiana, but for some reason as we came along, we went into a period where we weren't very active participants in the church. To my knowledge, Dad and Mom kept the standards of the church; we all did, but we didn't go very much. But thank heavens for a marvelous uncle, my dad's brother, and his wife, who worked on us and got us back in church. We weren't back into church very long (I remember I was nine) when I was asked to speak in sacrament—our main worship service.

Dad later became a wonderful priesthood leader in the church. But at the time, he didn't feel competent to help me put a talk together; and so he asked my Uncle Joseph to help me. Frankly, Uncle Joseph wrote out the talk and said, "Memorize it, and give it." At the time I was blessed with a good memory, and I did memorize it. I remember sitting in the stand looking out at what seemed to me to be about 5,000 people. It was probably about 100, but it seemed like 5,000 for a nine year old. I remember walking gingerly up to the pulpit and feeling very unstable.

I remember the feelings of hoping I could just get through this without passing out. I remember, though, as the moments passed and as I spoke, that a quiet, and calm settled over me. The talk couldn't have been more than four or five minutes long—it probably was closer to three. But then suddenly I began realizing that something unusual was

4    Jacob 3:7 [4:6].

83

happening to me. As I spoke, the things about which I was speaking began to become clearer to me. I sensed that what I was talking about was real, and it was true. My uncle wrote a talk for me on Joseph Smith's first vision. The very first talk I ever gave was on the coming of the Father and the Son to the boy Joseph. When I sat down, I knew far more than when I stood up.

Through the years, while I have had my times of lapse in terms of not being the boy or the young man I should have been, I don't think I ever really wavered from that faith. I can say today that I know, and I knew as a nine year old. I know a whole lot more about the world of upstate New York and the revivalism of the day. I know a great deal more about the Second Great Awakening, and the great Methodist circuit riders, and all of that. But I don't think I know any stronger today than I knew as a nine year old that the dispensation and the fullness of times began with God's response to the simple prayer of an unlearned boy.

The years went by. When I was fourteen Mom and Dad both felt that it was time for me to receive a patriarchal blessing. So we went to the ancient patriarch. Dad drove me about 50 miles to the place where the patriarch lived. I was introduced to this total stranger, who laid his hands upon my head and proceeded to tell me about myself. I reread that patriarchal blessing a couple of months ago. Once again I was stunned by the fact that the spirit of prophecy had let this simple man who was totally unknown to me tell me all about myself, about my past, and about my future. Among the things he said was this: "You will enjoy every occasion of preaching this gospel and will present it unto those who live in many nations of this world."

He went on to say that I should study the gospel at great length, especially the record of the people that was kept upon plates of gold. He said that through my knowledge of this people and this book, it would be my privilege to help bring many people into the faith.

Again I remember our driving home. I had noticed that when we were finished, the patriarch asked if he could speak with my dad. Dad had served as his scribe during the blessing and had written it all down. Later the patriarch typed it up and sent it to us. But when he asked to speak to Dad I didn't know what that was about.

As we were driving home, Dad asked how I was feeling. I said, "Well, you know it felt really good." I didn't know what else to say.

Then Dad said, "You know, the patriarch said he was almost overcome." He said, "You should know I feel this tremendous need to tell you to be sure that your son studies the Book of Mormon."

Dad said, "Well, I will try to do so."

"No, Bishop, **you must see** that he studies the Book of Mormon. I just think your son will spend a lot of time teaching the Book of Mormon."

He couldn't have known those things save by the spirit of prophecy and revelation. I look back and realize so many, many things have been so closely connected with the sweet opportunities I have had all over the world to stand and bear witness of the significant moments of the Restoration.

I know by the power of the Holy Ghost that God lives. He is our heavenly Father. He is as close to us as we will allow Him to be. I know that His Only Begotten Son, Who was sent into the world to redeem the world, is Jesus of Nazareth. He is the Christ. He is the Only Begotten Son in the flesh. I know that there is no pain, no hunger, no fatigue, no feeling of abuse or neglect, no feelings of disappointment, no feelings of inadequacy, and no hurt that cannot be healed by the Great Physician. He is the Great Physician. I know that salvation is in Him, and in Him alone. That is my testimony. But a testimony must be brought up to date; it must be current.

And my witness—a witness that is as strong to me as the witness that I have that God and Christ live and govern in our lives—is the witness that They did indeed appear to a boy, the prophet Joseph Smith. The angels were sent from the courts of glory to bestow priesthood powers; the church was organized under the direction of prophetic leadership; the Book of Mormon with latter day revelation all stand as witnesses that God loves His children of all ages; and He still speaks. Thus I do like Joseph said—believe all that God has revealed, and all that He does now reveal. And I do believe with all of my soul that He will yet reveal many great and important things pertaining to the kingdom of God.

I sense a bit of the parting of the veil. I sense the Lord is pleased with what has happened, and I sense that much, much more will happen. The work is in His hands, and my trust is in Him. I bear my witness that He will, in fact, bring to pass His purposes, in the name of Jesus Christ the Lord.

---

# Commentary

The testimony of Jesus is the spirit of prophecy. Those who have embraced the message couched within the Book of Mormon discover that page after page illuminates this testimony: *"We talk of Christ, we rejoice in Christ, we preach of Christ, we prophesy of Christ."*[5] We are persuaded to rely *"wholly upon the merits of him who is mighty to save"*[6] while it commends us to *"seek this Jesus of whom the prophets and apostles have written."*[7]

When Joseph Smith, Jr., went to the grove, the curtain was parted. God spoke to him in articulate, discernible, and unmistakably human words: *"This is my beloved Son; hear Him."*[8] This prophetic spirit has continued and is manifest among all those who love the latter-day work, disclosing to us that the work is in His hands, and He will, in fact, bring to pass His purposes. Our divine destiny is tied to this testimony of Jesus. It will eventually be the mechanism that repairs the breach, as He

---

5    2 Nephi 11:48 [25:26].
6    2 Nephi 13:28 [31:19].
7    Ether 5:41 [12:41].
8    *Times and Seasons,* Vol. 3:748, Independence Press, Independence, Missouri.

parts the veil to weld His Saints together, enabling the Restoration to reveal this testimony of Jesus to the world.

The testimony of Jesus is also the spirit of the Restoration that will ultimately bring to fruition the completion of the Marvelous Work and a Wonder. May we not only love the Book of Mormon but also cherish all those who embrace it, as we live out the dream of a prophetic people with a divine destiny, as He reveals to us the way.

---

*And thus they did retain a hope through faith, unto eternal salvation, relying upon the spirit of prophecy, which spake of those things to come.* [9]

---

9    Alma 14:77 [25:16].

# 15

# Fractal-like

*And they were converted unto the Lord, and were united unto the church of Christ, and thus the people of that generation were blessed, according to the word of Jesus.*[1]

What is a fractal? The *Oxford Dictionary* defines it this way:

> A curve or geometrical figure, each part of which has the same statistical character as the whole. They are useful in modeling structures (such as snowflakes) in which similar patterns recur at progressively smaller scales, and in describing partly random or chaotic phenomena such as crystal growth and galaxy formation.[2]

Fractals show us that similar patterns reoccur at progressively smaller scales. The word itself comes from the Latin *fract* meaning "broken." According to mathematics, fractals can describe everything from crystals to galaxies. Larger structures can be broken down into smaller and smaller ones, *ad infinitum*. Conversely, small structures can be expanded to larger ones into infinity. Fractals share

1    3 Nephi 13:36 [28:23].
2    https://en.oxforddictionaries.com/definition/fractal

the property of being self-similar, *i.e.*, that arbitrarily small pieces of them replicate the whole. More generally, we know that many objects found in nature have a kind of self-similarity—small pieces of them look similar to the whole. Some examples are clouds, waves, ferns, broccoli and cauliflower. We call these objects fractal-like.

Fractal-like objects are made up of pieces that are similar, or close in appearance—and so we say they look very much alike. We recognize that although two stalks of broccoli may look very similar, they are not exact replicas of each other. They are, nevertheless, self-similar—a small piece of one stock looks like some other broccoli.

This is the pattern we discover in the Restoration. The various churches emerging following the death of Joseph Smith have been broken or fractured off. The unique thing to remember, however, is that the Restoration churches look quite similar. They have reproduced or fractaled over and over again. They often claim distinction from one another—but at their core they adhere to many common beliefs and are fractal-like, *i.e.*, comparable, analogous or related much like the fractal-like objects discovered in nature.

Most people outside the Restoration would agree with this assessment. Perhaps when you mention you believe in the Book of Mormon, like me you have heard someone say, "Oh, you are a *Mormon*."

I like to reply by saying to such individuals, "Do you believe in the *Bible*?" If they respond in the affirmative, I then say, "That's good. So, let's see, does that make you a *Bible*?" This exchange generally leaves them puzzled. Nevertheless there is a great measure of truth in that statement.

We who embrace the Book of Mormon are fractal-like, similar, analogous, or related. We embrace the common idea of continuing revelation, a divinely restored church with an intercessory priesthood, the restoration of the house of Israel, and the building of a Holy City, etc. We may be different stalks of broccoli, but we are not cauliflower.

We are not part of Catholicism or Protestantism; instead we are Restorationists. Our commonalities should be embraced. The world can see us more clearly than the Saints see themselves; they recognize our unique and common beliefs as setting us apart, as self-similar. Perhaps we should, too.

---

Friendship is one of the grand fundamental
principles of Mormonism.[3]

§

### The Eyes of the Blind Shall See

*And in that day shall the deaf hear the words of the book; and the eyes
of the blind shall see out of obscurity and out of darkness.*[4]

### Sister Mary Fowler
### Reorganized Church of Jesus Christ of Latter Day Saints

Sister Mary Fowler had two sons, Asa and Robert, that were working to fix an acetylene gas leak at the Stiffel and Freeman safe manufacturer in Philadelphia, Pennsylvania, on December 7, 1909. The brick building had been cleared of all people because it contained sizeable amounts of flammable and explosive materials aside from the gas leak. A careless workman said, as he entered the room: "May I strike this match?" and striking it as he said so. Asa (George Asa) was killed instantly in the vault. Robert was buried under the ruins of the shop's safes, bricks, dust, and cinders.

A policeman soon came to Mary Fowler's home and told her to "Go right down to the hospital and claim the body of George Asa Fowler. He is dead."

Brother Walter Smith then came to the Fowler home and Mary asked

3  *Teachings of the Prophet Joseph Smith*, Joseph Fielding Smith, p. 316, Deseret Books, Salt Lake City, Utah, 1976.
4  2 Nephi 11:155 [27:29].

him: "How is Robert?"

He said: "Robert is in a bad condition."

Then I asked Brother Smith: "Has he been administered to?"

He said: "Yes, I have administered to him."

Mary asked: "What is the matter with him?"

Brother Smith replied: "I think his back is broken."

"What else is the matter with him?"

"His eyes are blown out."

"What else?"

"His eardrums are burst."

Mary replied: "Then I want you to tell me truly, is he living?"

Brother Smith said: "Yes, he is living, but I have no hope to tell you whatever."

"Well," she said, "that is a good bit to be thankful for—that he is living."

Then Brother Smith turned to her and said, "Shall I go get some neighbors to stay with you?"

She replied: "No, Brother Smith, I don't wish them."

"Shall I stay with you?"

Mary answered: "No, thank you, I want to be alone with my God."

"Very well," he said, "then I will go."

Mary's account of what happened next follows.

And as he went out, I knelt down by a chair and commenced to pray: "Dear Father, Thou hast taken one of my beloved ones unto thyself. In this Thou art welcome, for I know that my children are only loaned to me for a time. But this other loved one whose body is broken is now living at the gates of death, for whom I beseech Thee that in Thy great mercy Thou wilt heal him and return him unto me once more, whole in mind and body, that I may be able to bear with courage the heavy cross laid upon me." Of course, my prayer was much longer, but this is the substance of it.

From the moment I first knelt down, and all during the prayer, I was conscious of a being standing beside me. And although I saw no one, and my grief was too deep for tears, I felt his presence was strong enough to pierce through the wall of midnight blackness that had come upon me. I knew without doubt that a heavenly messenger was beside me listening to my pleading. When this fact was made fully known to me, the messenger spoke, a voice clear and distinct, "Thy son shall be made whole."

How can I explain the wonderful peace and gladness that swept over me and eased my sorrowing soul.

My husband had gone to the hospital with Brother Walter Smith and A. D. Angus and John Zimmerman, Sr., along. The three administered again to Robert. The boy's father and Brother Smith remained at the hospital all night. While they were there, the specialist said to my husband; "You ought to pray for the boy's death, for his back is broken, his eardrums are burst, and his eyes are gone. Besides all that; he is burned to a crisp and will be a fright to look at, if he ever recovers."

My husband made answer: "Do all you can for him and try to save his life, if possible, for this is the only hope my wife has, that she can come here and see her boy."

Early the next morning my husband went again to the hospital. Brother Smith was there before him. As the boy's father entered, the doctor met him at the door, and said: "Mr. Fowler, what color of eyes did your boy have?"

"Dark brown," my husband answered.

Then the doctor said: "If I didn't believe miracles were done away with, I would say that there was one of the greatest miracles wrought here last night that ever was wrought on this earth—yes, even when Christ was here!—because this morning he has the prettiest brown eyes that I have ever seen. Last night I could have taken an oath there was not an eye in his head, for I myself cleaned out his eye sockets, and I took a handful of brick dust and cinders out of each eye socket, and his empty eye bags were laying on either cheek. I don't pretend I don't know anything about it, but I can't understand it."

Upon this statement Brother Smith asked the doctor if he would give him a written testimony of this occurrence. The doctor hung his head for a minute and then said: "If I would give a written statement of this happening, I could not hold my job three weeks."

Robert's body began to heal in a miraculous way very quickly.

One day I arrived at the hospital, and the nurse addressed me: "O, Mrs. Fowler, I want you to see your boy. Just before you came in, I removed the mask [the scabs of the burns]. Come see his face—it's like a baby's—not a scar on it!!!"

When I beheld his face, I found the nurse had spoken the truth. There was not one mark where the burns had been healed.

Robert was in the hospital only 18 days, for we had the pleasure of having him by Christmas. The young people of the church here welcomed him home with a shower of fruit.

It was not long until Robert was as strong and well as he was before the accident; in fact, he was better. For before he was hurt, he had to wear glasses, as his eyes were not very strong; and it was quite some time until he needed them again—his line of work being rather hard on his eyes.[5]

There are several people still alive today who knew Robert Fowler and heard his testimony and that of his family.

**Sister Elizabeth Muskellunge**
**The Church of Jesus Christ (Bickertonite)**

---

5    *Testimony of a Mother in Israel*, Mary Fowler, pp. 6–10, Palenque Press, Independence, Missouri, 2013.

As with many evangelistic works in their early stages, miracles marked the beginning of the work in Muncey, Canada. There was an old blind woman who would attend regularly. Her name was Elizabeth Muskellunge. Her nephew, Angus De Leary, brought her to church every Sunday.

One Sunday (circa 1936), she requested baptism. Brother Matthew Miller, who was in charge at that time, performed the baptism. As our new sister was immersed into the waters of the Thames River and began to come out of the water, Brother Miller wiped the water from her face with his hand. Suddenly Sister Elizabeth shouted. "I see a hand!" We who were witnessing this baptism were shocked and amazed as we watched her running out of the water, [with] her eyes wide open. "I can see! I can see!" she repeated. She was dancing for joy. There were tears of joy, and songs of praise filled the air.

The news spread fast. Sister Muskellunge had been blind for 16 years. Some were doubtful at the phenomenon, but some praised God. Many came to visit her, considering what had happened [to be] a miracle. Others only thought of it as a coincidence or a temporary situation, but Sister Elizabeth could see well enough to thread a needle. Several additional baptisms resulted from this miracle.[6]

## Brother R. C. Evans
## The Reorganized Church of Jesus Christ of Latter Day Saints

*The Lord appointed other seventy also, and sent them two and two before his face, into every city and place where he himself would come. And he said unto them ... into whatsoever city ye enter, and they receive you, eat such things as are set before you; And heal the sick that are therein, and say, The kingdom of God is come nigh unto you.[7]*

On Thursday, December 1, 1887, I (Elder R. C. Evans) went to the home of Brother and Sister George Walker. Brother Walker had

---

6    *A History of the Church of Jesus Christ* [Bickertonite], Vol. 2, pp. 437–438.
7    Luke 10:1–9.

been working on a new Catholic church [building] in Chatham, Ontario, and had got some kind of cement with lime in his eyes.

They went for the doctor; but by the time the physicians reached him, his eyes were literally burned out. I was informed by Sister Walker, in the presence of her husband, that the eyeballs were burned away. The doctor had hard work to get the lids open wide enough to see the eyes. And where the eyes once were, there were red lumps a little larger than wintergreen berries. The doctor said there was no hope of his ever seeing again.

George Walker was in a room blindfolded when I arrived. He had been blind for several weeks. We talked for some time. All of a sudden silence reigned; and I heard a voice say, "He who spat upon the clay can heal this man today." The Spirit of the Lord rested upon me in power. I walked over to Brother Walker, led him to the lounge, laid my hands on his head, and prayed for just a moment. A power rested upon me; and I said, "In the name of Jesus Christ, I say unto thee, receive thy sight." I took my hands off his head. He sat up, opened his eyes, and did see. I bear my testimony to this in the name of Jesus Christ, before whom I must appear.[8]

———————————

*And whoso shall ask it in my name, in faith, they shall cast out devils; they shall heal the sick; they shall cause the blind to receive their sight, and the deaf to hear, and the dumb to speak, and the lame to walk.*[9]

———————————

8    *Autumn Leaves*, p. 513, M. Walker, Editor and Publisher, Lamoni, Iowa, November 1890.
9    D&C 34:3c, [35:9], BofC 37:10.

# 16

# Wheel of Fortune

*I beheld till the thrones were cast down, and the Ancient of days did sit, whose garment was white as snow, and the hair of his head like the pure wool; his throne was like the fiery flame, and his wheels as burning fire.*[1]

The typical bicycle wheel is made up of a rim suspended with tensioned spokes around a center. The spokes attach alternately on the right and left sides of the hub. The spokes on the right side pull the wheel to the right, and those attached to the left side of the hub pull the wheel to the left. The tension created from the spokes on each side holds the wheel straight or true. If all the spokes were attached to the same side, the wheel would not spin true or straight.

Within the Restoration, as advocates for and believers in the Book of Mormon and the angel message, we are all attached to the same hub. But our spokes may be on a different side of the hub from another's

---

1    Daniel 7:9.

spokes, *i.e.*, another branch of the churches of the Restoration. What we fear from our differences may actually allow the latter-day work to stay true or straight, until the Lord decides to replace the spoked wheel (the various organizations or churches) with a new wheel (a living organism; the Body of Christ) that can allow the Saints to complete the journey as we roll down Zion's road.

In our analogy, the differences in tension and its fastening to the hub can be characterized by the various gifts and tendencies associated with each branch of the Restoration. Within the latter-day churches, we find many common denominators as well as some variations in organization, administration, spiritual manifestations, manner of worship, size, missionary approach, ecclesiastical zeal, and historical inquiry. These variations illustrate the different emphasis on varying aspects of the latter-day work. This is further illustrated in the family of stringed instruments. The sound these instruments produce is directly tied to the length, thickness, and amount of tension applied to each string. Without these differences, the melody that moves us will not be heard and appreciated.

In any sort of team sports, players with different skills, talents, or abilities assume different roles. Each is essential to the overall success of the team. The dynamics of how a team functions is based on how these various parts interact and work together to achieve success. The variances between the Restoration churches at times—while viewed as a source of tension—are essential to better equip us to carry out the great commission to evangelize the world and zionize the church.

These unique characteristics developed in separate organizations since 1844 will eventually allow each portion of the Restoration to become the recipients of the others' rich treasures, as the church gives birth to the Holy City and makes herself ready for the coming of the Bridegroom—for which all of creation waits. May we continue striving for unity, even as we learn to appreciate our dissimilarities and how the God of Israel has used the various spokes of the wheel to keep the

Restoration true, straight and balanced, and her melody on key with her assortment of strings.

---

*And it came to pass that the Lord of the vineyard said again unto his servant, Look hither, and behold another branch also, which I have planted; behold that I have nourished it also, and it hath brought forth fruit.*[2]

§

## The Ice Moved

*I, Nephi, said unto my father, I will go and do the things which the Lord hath commanded, for I know that the Lord giveth no commandments unto the children of men, save he shall prepare a way for them that they may accomplish the thing which he commandeth them.*[3]

### Sister Anna and Brother Clarence Kirkpatrick
### The Church of Jesus Christ (Bickertonite)

Anna was very afraid of water; she was pregnant with our first daughter who was due in two to three weeks. She was having a real battle. One morning about 5:30 a.m., she told me she had won the battle with Satan. That was Sunday morning. Anna said, "We will go to Church and get baptized today."

The temperature that day was about 20° above zero when we arrived at the lagoon on the Monongahela River. The river was frozen solid. While they were trying to get a hole broken in the ice big enough to baptize us, a huge tugboat, pulling six huge barges of coal, came down the river. The huge paddle, pushing and churning, caused such a large wake that it broke up the ice. It caused the ice to move out from the bank away from the shore.

Brother Clyde Gibson took us into the water and baptized us. As we left the water, the ice floated back toward shore. While we were

2    Jacob 3:67 [5:24].
3    1 Nephi 1:65 [3:7].

standing on the bank of the river, Anna opened her eyes and saw a beam of light as bright as the sun, in the shape of a funnel, spread over all of us.[4]

### Brother John F. Sheehy
### The Reorganized Church of Jesus Christ of Latter Day Saints

In the winter of 1913–14, we were living in Corea, Maine. We had been holding meetings for several months, and finally nine young people requested baptism. It was in the middle of an extremely cold winter, all the way from 20° to 35° below zero. Snow was piled everywhere.

Finally came the Sunday of the baptisms. They had been advertised, and people gathered into Corea from miles around to see what they called a "Mormon baptism." Many people thought it foolish to baptize in the cold waters of the Atlantic in winter. "Why not wait until summer or warmer weather?" they asked. But actually it wouldn't have made much difference in the temperature of the water, for the water in the state of Maine is always cold—very cold—whether it's July or January.

We arranged for the baptismal service to be at two o'clock on Sunday afternoon. On Friday the temperature dropped, and the harbor was completely frozen over. Even the Atlantic Ocean was frozen out beyond the islands, and we wondered what we should do. On Saturday it was still cold, and the harbor was a solid mass of ice. On Sunday morning it was still the same. At one o'clock on Sunday afternoon it was still a solid mass of ice.

Brother James Clark was the only male member of the Church who lived in Corea. He had been happy about the baptisms, but now he was very concerned. How could we baptize in a harbor covered with ice? I said to Brother Clark, "There is nothing that we can do about this. All we can do is get ready. If at two o'clock the harbor is still full of ice, then we'll have to wait until the weather changes and it's more convenient."

---

4 *A History of the Church of Jesus Christ* [Bickertonite], Vol. 2, p. 111.

Those who were to be baptized and a few friends gathered in the home of Sister Francis. We bowed our heads and had prayer. We told the Lord about the situation and reminded Him that there was nothing we could do. We asked for His help and guidance in the matter and asked that He give us wisdom so that we wouldn't do anything foolish. It wasn't long after we had prayer that Guy Francis, a young fisherman, asked Brother Clark, "Did you hear that?"

"Yes, I heard it."

"Hear what?" I asked. "I didn't hear anything."

They said, "Why, the wind changed!" They had heard the wind change. We looked out the window, and it wasn't long before the ice broke up and started to move out of the harbor.

I said, "What a strange thing this is!"

Brother Clark said, "Yes, stranger than you realize." We waited about ten minutes, and at two o'clock the ice had all moved out of the harbor. Brother Clark said, "We'd better have our baptisms and waste no time."

We went to the shore and had the usual ceremony. We sang hymns and offered prayer. But the crowd that was making a lot of noise to make fun of us was hushed to silence. They were very surprised to see the ice move out of the harbor. We had the baptisms. Brother Guy Francis was about nineteen, a strong young man of the sea, so I baptized him last. As he and I walked out into the water, he said, "You'd better hurry."

"Why?" I asked.

"The wind's changed again," He said. "The ice is coming back into the harbor." I looked, and sure enough, the ice was moving back rapidly. Before I immersed him, we braced our feet and with both hands shoved a big ice cake out of the way. As we walked out of the water, the ice followed us to the shore. Within a few minutes the harbor was completely frozen again, and it remained that way for over a week. We should be ever grateful that we believe in and worship a God who hears and answers our prayers and gives us direction in our work when we are laboring for Him.[5]

---

*And it came to pass that the Lord of the vineyard said again unto his servant, Look hither, and behold another branch also, which I have planted; behold that I have nourished it also, and it hath brought forth fruit.*[6]

---

5    *Brightly Beams Our Father's Mercy*, pp. 93–95, compiled by George Gross and
     published privately in Missouri, 2000.
6    Jacob 3:67 [5:24].

# 17

# The Truth

*And if ye shall ask with a sincere heart, with real intent, having faith in Christ, he will manifest the truth of it unto you, by the power of the Holy Ghost; and by the power of the Holy Ghost, ye may know the truth of all things.[1]*

A peasant went to town on a certain occasion. Looking into a shop window, he saw a mirror—the first mirror he had ever seen. And when he looked into that mirror, what do you suppose he saw? Why, the very picture of his father as he remembered him as a young man. He thought it was the spirit of his father; and so he got together all the money he had, purchased that mirror, and took it home. He carried it into the attic and built a little altar to put the mirror on. Every day he would make offerings and pray before that altar, look into the mirror, and the spirit of his father would look back at him.

---

1    Moroni 10:5.

All would have gone well except that this man had a wife who was curious, as women sometimes are (and men as well). She began to wonder why her husband went up into the attic every day and why he locked the door when he came down. So one day when her husband was gone, she climbed up into the attic, and found the mirror, and looked into it. And what do you suppose she saw? A young woman, and rather a good-looking woman too, she thought.

Now, she knew why her husband went into the attic every day. The perfidious wretch went up there to see that woman. So she went down the ladder; and when her husband came home, there was trouble. He insisted he saw his father in the mirror, and he told the truth. However, she said the thing that looked out at her was a woman—a young woman—and she, too, told the truth.

Finally, to settle the controversy, they decided to send for an old woman who was something of a sorceress; and so they brought her in. She was bent and crippled with age, but she climbed laboriously up the ladder and was gone a long time. When she came down, she said, "You are both fools. It is an old woman that is in the mirror." Then they all began to quarrel. The remarkable part of it is that, she, too, had told the truth. All told the truth just as they had seen it.

How much like the characters in our story the Scattered of the Restoration are. Often times we see what we want to see—what we are trained to see. Our perspectives are colored by the way we have been raised in the gospel. For too long the Saints have resisted looking in the mirror together.

What would have happened if twenty-five years prior to World War II all the babies born to the Germans were swapped at birth with those born to the British? The British would then be fighting for Hitler's Third Reich and the Germans would be fighting for the British. It all has to do with how we are taught.

What if our children in the Restored Gospel were placed in the homes of other branches of the Restoration and raised in their traditions? Evidences abound how the Holy Spirit has been manifest in a myriad of ways to heal the sick, speak in tongues, dream dreams, perform miracles, receive angelic ministry, and feel the warmth of the Holy Spirit confirming the legitimacy of the angel message in the different branches of the Restoration. Yet the conclusion, which most often unfolds, is since I read the Book of Mormon and received a witness of its authenticity, Joseph Smith must have been a prophet, and the person who handed me the book must be a representative of the one true church. Like the characters in our story, we are all telling the "truth" as it has come to us. Just like the characters in the story of the mirror, we have not perceived that others in the Restoration are also telling the "truth."

A new day is soon to dawn, when all the wrongs will be made right. The breach will be healed, and with a united voice we will join hands going forth in power to proclaim the everlasting gospel, calling Israel home, that the city may be built, and the bride made ready, adorned for the Bridegroom to usher in the peaceful reign. The prophetic voice will yet speak to all His Saints, inviting us to become one. Let us prepare for that day by praying that we may be permitted to help enrich the soil for the sowing of that seed, which will grow into the kingdom of God as we jointly look into the mirror to see His image there.

---

*And thus will I bring them together again, that they shall bring forth the natural fruit; and they shall be one.*[2]

§

### Sunday Miracle

*And he commanded them that they should observe the Sabbath day, and keep it holy, and also every day they should give thanks to the Lord their God.*[3]

---

2    Jacob 3:134 [5:68].
3    Mosiah 9:56 [18:23].

## Brother Lowell Fox
## The Church of Jesus Christ of Latter-day Saints

In 1946, a tannery was established for the LDS welfare program. Brother Lowell Fox who had studied tanning was placed in charge of the operation. Brother Fox wrote about a miracle the tannery experienced every week, which was brought to his attention the day following a holiday.

Upon returning to the tannery after the holiday, I found the hides being processed were spoiled, and we wondered what caused it. A careful check was made to see if these hides had been handled in a different way. They had been washed, cleaned, cut, and placed into large vats filled with limewater where they were to stay for four days. At the end of this time, the hair would come loose from the skins.

On regular workdays the hides were removed from the vats every twelve hours, the solution strengthened with fresh lime, stirred thoroughly, and the hides returned to the lime solution. This had not been done over the holiday. However, the change was never made on Sundays, and we had never found spoiled hides on Monday morning. That could not be the trouble! There seemed to be no reason for the spoiled hides.

All went well at the tannery until the next holiday when the incident repeated itself. Once more the hides spoiled. Not understanding why, we wrote the Technical Institution of New York to help us solve our problem. They verified the fact that while hides are soaking in the lime solution they must be stirred several times each day in order to keep them from spoiling during the time the hair is loosened; they must be taken from the vats every twelve hours while fresh lime is added to the solution.

This brought a strange fact to our minds: holidays are determined by man, and on these days just as on every week day, the hides need to have special care every twelve hours. Sunday is the day set aside by the Lord as a day of rest, and He makes it possible for us to rest from our labors as He has commanded. The hides at the tannery never spoil on Sundays. This is a modern-day miracle, a miracle that happens every weekend.[4]

---

# Commentary

The Sabbath was set apart each week for rest and worship. In the Old Testament, God's covenant people were commanded to keep the Sabbath on the seventh day of the week because God rested on the seventh day after He had created the heavens and the earth. Following the resurrection of our Lord—Jesus' disciples began observing the Lord's Day on the first day of the week—Sunday.[5] In the early days of the Restored Church, specific guidance was revealed to help the Saints understand as well as honor this day:

> *And that thou mayest more fully keep thyself unspotted from the world, thou shalt go to the house of prayer and offer up thy sacraments upon my holy day; for verily this is a day appointed unto thee to rest from thy labors, and to pay thy devotions unto the Most High; nevertheless thy vows shall be offered up in righteousness on all days, and at all times; but remember that on this, the Lord's day, thou shalt offer thine oblations, and thy sacraments, unto the Most High, confessing thy sins unto thy brethren, and before the Lord. And on this day thou shalt do none other thing, only let thy food be prepared with singleness of heart, that thy fasting may be perfect; or in other words, that thy joy may be full. Verily this is fasting and prayer; or, in other words, rejoicing and prayer.[6]*

There is a storied history regarding the observance of the Lord's Day, with many examples of blessings attendant to its observance. May the Scattered of the Restoration in their various plantings remember to honor this commandment that we may live within God's divine favor as

---

4    *Handbook for Guide Patrol Leaders* [Primary Manual, 1964], p. 37. www.lds. org/church/news/pure-religion-moment-sunday-miracle?lang=eng&_r=1
5    Mark 16:2, Acts 20:7.
6    D&C 59:3b [59:9–14] *The Evening and the Morning Star*, Vol. 1, No. 2, July 1832.

we long for the day when we shall see eye to eye when He brings again Zion, and we enter into God's seventh day of rest, the millennium.

———————————

*The whole earth is at rest, and is quiet: they break forth into singing.*[7]

7    2 Nephi 10:29 [24:7], Isaiah 14:7.

# 18

# The Linchpin

*For they were men of sound understanding, and they had searched the scriptures diligently, that they might know the word of God.[1]*

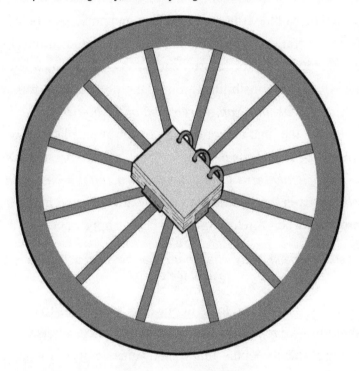

How important is the Book of Mormon? A linchpin exists to hold different parts or elements together, enabling them to function as a single unit. In the Restoration the Book of Mormon can be viewed as our linchpin to fasten the various Saints of the Restoration together. It preceded the restoration of the priesthood as well as the emergence of the church springing forth from the wilderness. It recounts in great detail the history of the Nephites and Lamanites, and to a lesser degree the Mulekites and Jaradites—even though none of these peoples ever held

---

1    Alma 12:4 [17:2].

the book in their hands. We may miss the point if we are not looking for it, but the book was written to and reserved for our day.

When Mormon abbreviated the many records creating the Book of Mormon, he abridged centuries of records, choosing those events, stories, sermons, experiences, and prophecies that would be most expedient[2] in empowering us to carry out the promises foretold within its pages. Nephi disclosed that he had received the assurance that those things which he would write would be kept and preserved, being handed down from generation to generation.[3] Both Enos[4] and Jarom[5] indicated they, too, were writing for future generations. Mormon, when coming to the end of his responsibilities, joined the prophetic chorus when he wrote, "*Yea, I speak unto you, ye remnant of the house of Israel,*"[6] while his son Moroni, the final author and depositor of the plates, saw our day and warned, "*Behold, I speak unto you as if ye were present, and yet ye are not. But behold, Jesus Christ hath shown you unto me, and I know your doing.*"[7] Even the realities of our day are reflected in the language of the prophets when foretelling of the book's appearance:

*Yea, it shall come in a day when there shall be great pollutions upon the face of the earth.*[8]

If the book was written to us in our day, to equip us to complete the work, shouldn't we read from this book daily? This exercise will enable the Saints to plumb its depths, that we may uncover its unfolding treasure of riches. Those riches will make us spiritually wealthy, magnifying those points of agreement on all things essential, and like a linchpin will hold the Saints from the various spokes or churches of the Restoration together as we roll down Zion's road.

---

2    3 Nephi 12:3 [26:9].
3    2 Nephi 11:40 [25:21].
4    Enos 1:23–26 [1:15–16].
5    Jarom 1:2.
6    Mormon 3:24 [7:1].
7    Mormon 4:45–47 [8:34-35].
8    Mormon 4:38 [8:31].

It is impossible to outgrow the Book of Mormon. It is impossible to have discovered all of its secret treasures.[9]

§

### The Day of Jubilee

*And there shall be one fold and one shepherd.*[10]

### Patrick S. McKay Sr.
### The Restoration Branch Movement

On Sunday morning June 19, 2013, I preached at one of our local Restoration Branches in Independence, Missouri. It was Pentecost Sunday. So I preached about the Feast of Weeks and how on that day God poured out His Spirit on the New Testament Church through the gift of tongues. I attempted to paint for the audience the significance of the feast days and their prophetic nature as they relate to the angel message. After citing several examples in our history where significant events have unfolded on these very days, I asked the Saints to consider as well as anticipate that God will yet reveal great things to us on these feast days. I bore testimony of how I believed God was soon to make bare His arm and heal the breach in the entire Restoration. I then concluded my remarks by quoting from an old Protestant song, "The Church's Jubilee" by Charles W. Naylor, circa 1920:

> For out of Babel God doth call
> His scattered Saints in one,
> To gather all one church compose,
> The body of His Son.
> O church of God, the day of jubilee
> Has dawned so bright and glorious for thee;
> Rejoice, be glad! Thy Shepherd has begun
> His long-divided flock again
> To gather into one.

---

9    *As One Crying from the Dust,* Brent Top, Preface p. 14, Deseret Books, Salt Lake City, Utah, 2014.
10   1 Nephi 7:58 [22:25].

111

That evening I received a text from a dear sister from the Church of Jesus Christ (Bickertonite) regarding an experience which transpired in Holiday, Florida, at the Forest Hills Branch of the Church of Jesus Christ. They were discussing a revelation which they had received two months earlier. Its content centered on the healing of the breach and how God would gather the Scattered of the Restoration. Then an individual stood and sang in the gift of tongues the chorus of "The Church's Jubilee." How remarkable! The very thing I had preached about transpired to sew hope among the believers of the Restoration. The gift of tongues was manifest on Pentecost Sunday, revealing our eventual fate as latter-day Saints. The God of Israel is moving to complete His work, to bring about His "*strange act.*"[11]

May we seek to cleanse our hands and purify our hearts, that we may be a part of this unfolding miracle as the day of Jubilee dawns.

---------------

*There were no ... manner of ites; but they were in one, the children of Christ, and heirs to the kingdom of God* [12]

### Dale E. Luffman
### The Community of Christ

*Were it not for these things, which have been kept and preserved by the hand of God, that we might read and understand of his mysteries, and have his commandments always before our eyes, that even our fathers would have dwindled in unbelief.*[13]

I still recall with a certain clarity times as a child when my family gathered around the kitchen table to color, cut, and prepare Book of Mormon flannelgraph figures and scenes. (Whiteboards and Power Point have replaced flannelgraph since that time.) I can still smell the crayons! My father, a convert to the gospel just a month before my

---

11   Isaiah 28:21.
12   4 Nephi 1:20 [1:17].
13   Mosiah 1:7 [1:5].

birth, had become quite knowledgeable of the Book of Mormon and was frequently asked to teach classes on the book. These classes included flannelgraph presentations. And we were his helpers.

As we cut and colored Lehi and his family, Samuel the Lamanite prophet, and other heroes and characters, my father would relate the Book of Mormon story to us. It seemed to me that I was right there with the adventures of the sons of Mosiah. Our family lived these stories. We then relived them as they were taught in the various congregations of the church in the state of Oregon.

The witness of the Book of Mormon was significant in bringing my father into the church. My mother had introduced him to the book. Then Seventy Arthur "Pete" Gibbs aided my father in discovering the message of the Book of Mormon, and the truth my father found in the book transformed his life.[14]

# Commentary

In Lucy Mack Smith's history she recalled events which took place in the evenings in the Smith home:

> Joseph would occasionally give us some of the most amusing recitals that could be imagined. He would describe the ancient inhabitants of this continent, their dress, mode of travel, their cities, their buildings, with every particular; their mode of warfare; and also their religious worship. This he would do with as much ease, seemingly, as if he had spent his whole life with them.[15]

The narrations which Joseph rehearsed were not "tall tales" that he fabricated for his family's amusement. It was information he had received from his tutor, the angel Moroni. These stories were used in much the same way as the flannelgraph to relate the history of the peoples of the Book of Mormon. These recitations revealed the adventures of

---

14 *The Book of Mormon's Witness to Its First Readers*, Dale Luffman, p. 1, Community of Christ Seminary Press, 2017.
15 *Joseph Smith the Prophet and His Progenitors*, Lucy Mack Smith, p. 92, Published by the Reorganized Church of Jesus Christ of Latter Day Saints, Lamoni, Iowa, 1912.

the former inhabitants of this land, allowing the Smith family to live these stories. They relived them again when the book was translated and published.

Today, the Scattered of the Restoration will both find as well as retain their strength coupled with the promise of a people united in our telling and retelling the story and message of the Book of Mormon.

———————————

I want it absolutely clear when I stand before the judgment
bar of God that I declared to the world ... that the
Book of Mormon is true.[16]

16   LDS Apostle Jeffery Holland, www.lds.org/general-conference/2009/10

# 19

# The Loom

*And the righteous shall have a perfect knowledge of their enjoyment, and their righteousness, being clothed with purity, yea, even with the robe of righteousness.*[1]

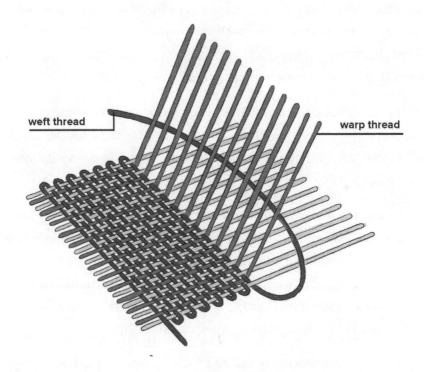

weft thread

warp thread

Most fabrics are woven or created on a loom with interlocking warp (the thread that is strung lengthwise on the loom) and weft (the thread that cuts across the warp fiber and interlocks with it).

Another type of textile is felt. Felt is a dense, non-woven fabric without any warp or weft. Instead, felted fabric is made from fibers with no threads. It is produced as these fibers are put together using heat, moisture, and pressure. This particular textile, although smooth

---

1    2 Nephi 6:35 [9:14].

and attractive, can be easily torn. It can figuratively forecast for us the various churches of the Restoration. We have all entered the "waters" of regeneration and felt the "warmth" of the Holy Spirit as we have been "pressed" into the work.

Our independent churches can be compared to this dense non-woven fabric that is flat, attractive, and smooth, but which lacks elasticity and limits our pliability. We all want to remain "true" to the original tenets of the gospel. We find it so difficult to interact with each other for fear that the fabric of our church may be torn by false beliefs and practices. As our critics combine to attack the angel message in our day, many Saints have been swept away because the fabric of "the church" has not been able to sufficiently protect or cover all of her children.

Each of the churches has told the story with its sanitized history and has left the Saints at times unable to answer the censures about our historical past with its seer stones, divining rods, angelic visitations, and the "golden Bible."

There are many within the fabric of the Restoration who have the testimony of the authenticity of the latter-day light. It is God's purpose to now begin to unite us that we might accomplish the thing He has called us to do, that we might witness the completion of His "*strange act*"[2] when "*Zion shall flourish, and the glory of the Lord shall be upon her;*"[3] and He pours out His Spirit upon all flesh.[4]

God is in the process of taking the differences in the Restoration, the warp and the woof, and sewing us together, that the gospel message may easily cover and protect all the Saints as well as rescue those who have fallen away. He can make us beautiful, pliable, supple, and free from rending so that we no longer will be divided and lament the fact that we have not been able to produce the kingdom of Zion. Let us be reminded of what the Saints were told in the early days of the Restoration:

---

2    Isaiah 28:21.
3    D&C 64:8a [64:41].
4    D&C 92:1c [95:4].

*Behold … I say unto you, Be one; and if ye are not one*
*ye are not mine.*[5]

---

*Wherefore, if God so clothe the grass of the field, which today is, and*
*tomorrow is cast into the oven, even so will he clothe you, if ye are not*
*of little faith.*[6]

§

### God's Power to Heal

*Is any sick among you? Let him call for the elders of the church; and let*
*them pray over him, anointing him with oil in the name of the Lord: And*
*the prayer of faith shall save the sick, and the Lord shall raise him up;*
*and if he have committed sins, they shall be forgiven him.*[7]

## Brother Kevin Murphy
## The Church of Jesus Christ (Bickertonite)

There were a number of Saints at the old Tampa Mission cleaning the place up. One of the sisters was making coffee for the group. She poured a couple of cups then turned to hand a cup to another of the sisters. As she had her back to a little toddler, he reached up, grabbed the other cup of steaming coffee, and spilled it down onto his face and chest. We all jumped when he screamed from the pain. We pulled off his shirt to see that his face and chest were bright red from the burn.

The one elder present grabbed the holy oil, placed a drop on the boy's chest, and began to pray. We that were there watched as all the redness moved into a little circle where the oil had been placed. The boy then ran off and went about playing as if nothing happened. That boy was my son. Thank God for His mercy.[8]

---

5    *The Evening and the Morning Star*, Vol.1, No. 8, p. 60, January 1833.
6    3 Nephi 6:8 [13:30].
7    James 5:14–15.
8    Personal correspondance to the author.

## Sister Joy McKay
## The Reorganized Church of Jesus Christ of Latter Day Saints

One evening shortly after I was married, I decided to make vegetable soup using a pressure cooker we had received as a wedding gift. I chose to use the pressure cooker to speed up the process. I turned the stove on high, and after several minutes I realized the pressure release valve was not jiggling. I had never used a pressure cooker before so was unfamiliar with its use. I decided to open the lid to see what the problem was. As I did so, it burst as if a bomb had gone off. The lid flew out of my hands and into the family room; and the soup exploded on me, scalding my face, neck, chest, and arms.

Patrick heard the explosion and came running to the kitchen. He saw I was beet red. We immediately called for the elders to come and administer to me. Following the administration, one of the elders poured consecrated olive oil on my blistered skin. The next day upon rising, I found no evidence that my skin had been burned. I will be forever thankful for His protection over me and grateful for the authority bestowed on God's servants.[9]

------------

*And they were healed by the power of the Lamb of God.*[10]

------------

9    Personal testimony of the author's wife.
10   1 Nephi 3:85 [11:31].

# 20

# Xylem and Phloem

*And we called the place Bountiful, because of its much fruit.*[1]

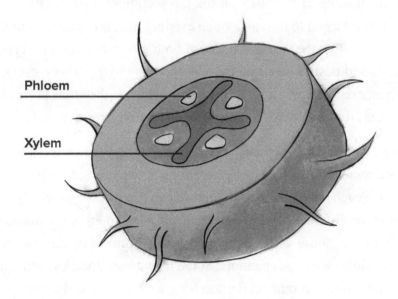

Phloem

Xylem

T he Apostle Paul in his Roman letter described how the branches of the house of Israel were broken off and wild branches were grafted in their place. He explained the transfer of the gospel to the Gentiles following the time of Christ.[2] The Book of Mormon elucidates for us how this became operative:

> *Behold, the branches of the wild tree hath taken hold of the moisture of the root thereof, that the root thereof hath brought forth much strength.*[3]

In the Book of Mormon, we are also taught that prior to this time some young and tender branches were removed from the mother tree (the house of Israel) and grafted in various parts of the Lord's vineyard.

---

1   1 Nephi 5:67 [17:6].
2   Romans 11:11–25.
3   Jacob 3:54 [5:18].

Some were placed in a choice land, and others in poor spots, and still others in spots poorer yet.[4] Because Nephi reminds us, *"I did liken all scriptures unto us that it might be for our profit and learning,"*[5] we, the Scattered of the Restoration may, like Nephi, apply the parable of Zenos to the churches of the Restoration following the death of Joseph Smith, Jr.

In the grafting of various fruit trees, a section of a stem with some leaf buds is attached to the stock of an existing tree. It is placed onto the stock plant so that the vascular tissue of both pieces line up. The xylem then pulls and pushes water up through the plant to the leaves, causing photosynthesis with the sun creating sugar, which is then transported by the phloem from the leaves to nourish the rest of the tree.

This gives us a great opportunity to consider how we should interact with one another. You see, as Restorationists, we are not each other's enemy. We each have special fruit that we can produce. Figuratively, the fruit from the different branches of the Restoration could be compared to stone fruits; *i.e.*, those with a large seed inside. Some of us may produce peaches, while others make plums. Some may create cherries, delicious apricots, or sweet nectarines. For too long we have worked against one another, twisting our branches around the other, preventing some from growing. We surmise that if they are not producing the same type of fruit that we produce, then we think they must be doing it wrong—that God would never honor their fruit. So we try to grow over them, blocking the sunlight, choking them off.

You can't grow every kind of fruit on the same tree, but you can graft related fruits on the same tree. The various churches of the Restoration all have received their nourishment from the main root; therefore, we are all a part of the same tree. I recently saw an advertisement for a fruit salad tree that can grow up to six different types of fruit all on one tree. These fruit trees are multi-grafted trees with different fruits from the same family (like stone fruits) grafted together on one tree. You can't

4    Jacob 3:63–68 [5:21–25].
5    1 Nephi 6:5 [19:23].

grow every kind of fruit on the same tree, but you can graft related fruits on the same trees.

We, as believers in the fullness of the gospel, are all a part of the latter-day glory. We all claim a divinely restored priesthood with the power to remit sin in the waters of regeneration, to bestow the gift of the Holy Ghost, and heal the sick by the laying on of hands. Angels have lodged in our branches to protect, comfort, guide, and confirm to us the truth. The gifts of the Spirit, such as prophecy, dreams, visions, tongues and their interpretation have graced our assemblies. The testimony of the Book of Mormon undergirds all we profess with its remarkable Christology. Each group preaches, prays, and longs for the restoration of the house of Israel and the redemption of Zion. How can this be? Simple. We have all been connected to the main root. Our spiritual xylem has been transporting the living waters of the testimony of Jesus throughout our various branches of the church, causing photosynthesis with the Son; creating revelation, which the phloem or elders have carried back through the branches to maintain the spirit, power, and promise of the angel message. This process has been enacted over and over again by the men of the ministry as they preach and teach the everlasting gospel to nourish the Saints, illustrating that we are all a part of the same plant.

Naturally, our separation has caused us to develop some traditions and gifts that are different. When the Holy Spirit grafts us all back together, we will each have unique or specialized gifts or fruits to strengthen and enliven the body of Christ, thus equipping us with a greater ability to testify of the Lord Jesus and the fruit of His kingdom.

---

*And it came to pass that the Lord of the vineyard said again unto his servant, Look hither, and behold another branch also, which I have planted; behold that I have nourished it also, and it hath brought forth fruit.*[6]

---

6    Jacob 3:67 [5:24].

§

## God Is Good and Mindful of His Saints

*And it shall come to pass, that before they call, I will answer; and while they are yet speaking, I will hear.*[7]

### Brother Frank Natoli
### The Church of Jesus Christ (Bickertonite)

A s a newly ordained elder in the Church of Jesus Christ, I was instructed to always carry a small bottle of blessed oil with me, in case someone contacted me and asked to be anointed.[8]

One morning, I awoke, got ready for work, ate my breakfast, and got in my car to go to work. Before I walked out the door, I touched the outside of my pants to feel for my little bottle of oil. But I had forgotten it. So I went back into my room, placed it in my pants pocket and left for work. The sun was just coming up, brightening the sky as I approached a red light just around the corner from my home. It was early, and I felt as if I was the only one on the road. I stopped at the red light, like we all do, and patiently waited for it to turn green.

When I saw the light turn, I pressed down on the accelerator. But the car didn't move. Strange, I thought, what's wrong with my car? Then suddenly, a speeding car flew through the intersection, running a red light, never coming close to slowing down! My heart began to pound, and I immediately knew that I could have been killed or badly hurt had my car responded as it always did when I hit the gas pedal. With my heart still pounding, I sat quietly at the intersection, thanking God for sparing my life.

You may be wondering what significance the blessed oil played. I wasn't sick and no one called me to anoint them. But when I looked

---

7    Isaiah 65:24.
8    James 5:14–16.

122

down at my pants, I saw a small stain about one inch in diameter. It wasn't there when I left my house because I recalled looking at my pants and my pocket. I looked again and realized the spot was exactly where I placed my little bottle of blessed oil (you know, the one I almost forgot). I reached awkwardly into my pocket and found that the bottle had a crack in it, and that it leaked!

Now my heart was really pounding and tears came to my eyes. I'd been carrying it with me for months and it had never had a crack in it. I knew the Lord was simply reminding me that His protection was upon me. Even before I called on Him, He answered.[9]

## Brother Fred Lamar
## The Reorganized Church of Jesus Christ of Latter Day Saints

Althea Lamar, a Baptist, married Joseph Thomas, a member of the Reorganized Church of Jesus Christ of Latter Day Saints. Her father was quite disturbed when she joined the church. He had asked the Lord which of the two churches was right, but he received no answer. Subsequent to this time, her father was lying in the hospital with a broken hip, and he was still concerned. In prayer, he asked the Lord if Joseph Smith was a true prophet. In a dream, a very large book opened before him; and he began reading. As he read, the leaves were turned for him without any effort on his part. He read page after page that proved to him Joseph Smith was a true prophet.

This experience gave him a desire to be baptized. When Althea came to visit him that afternoon, he requested baptism. She was very happy, but she wondered how they could baptize him with a broken hip. When her husband came in from work that evening, she talked it over with him and asked his advice. He said, "We will just make arrangements to comply with his request." So the plans were laid, and the date was set. Brother Fred Lamar had to be carried down into the water to be

---

9    The Gospel Blog/The Church of Jesus Christ, July 13, 2015.

baptized. When he was baptized, he jumped up, and walked out of the water. He was instantly healed![10]

---

# Commentary

M iracles, signs, and wonders accompanied the everlasting gospel when the church first sprang forth out of the wilderness. There continue to be manifestations within the various branches of the Restored Church. These experiences confirm for its members that they are where God has placed them. Remember, Nephi did liken all Scripture unto his people that it might be for their profit and learning;[11] and so, too, can we. Like the parable of Zenos and the restoration of the house of Israel, the various branches of God's church will be grafted back into one body. God is good and mindful of all His Saints. He has been and continues to be setting in motion those events, disclosing His divine will to weld us back together as the day of Zion's redemption draws near.

---

*And it came to pass that the people of Zarahemla, and of Mosiah, did unite together.[12]*

---

10   *True Restoration Adventures*, Compiled by Clara Thomas, pp. 97–98, Sionita School, Inc., Bates City, Missouri, 1986..
11   1 Nephi 6:5 [19:23].
12   Omni 1:34 [1:19].

# 21

# The Mustard Seed

*Truth shall spring out of the earth; and righteousness shall look down from heaven.*[1]

Brother Joseph Smith, Jr., when writing on the gathering, referred to the parable of the mustard seed having an allusion to the kingdom of God, which should be set up just previous to or at the time of harvest:

> Let us take the Book of Mormon, which a man took and hid in his field, securing it by his faith, to spring up in the last days, or in due time; let us behold it coming forth out of the ground, which is indeed accounted the least of all seeds, but behold it branching forth, yea, even towering, with lofty branches and God-like majesty, until it, like the mustard seed, becomes the greatest of all herbs. And it is truth, and it has sprouted and come forth out of the earth, and righteousness begins to look down from heaven, and God is sending down His powers, gifts, and angels to lodge in the branches thereof. The kingdom of heaven is like unto a mustard seed.[2]

---

1     Psalm 85:11.
2     *Latter Day Saints' Messenger and Advocate,* Vol. 2, No. 3, p. 227, Kirtland, Ohio, December 1835.

Here we have a powerful simile of those events unfolding in the latter days. The prophetic imagery is stirring, with the comparison of the mustard seed to the emergence of the Book of Mormon, designating it as a herald of things to come. The spectacle of its "*springing up*," (1823–1827) "*coming forth*," (1827–1830) and "*branching forth*," (1830–peaceful reign) as Joseph stated, through its role as a focal point in signaling divine activity seems to suggest that its coming forth was as significant as what it reveals.

Because of the coming forth of the book, we can testify that God has spoken from on high. We can declare with assurance that we believe in a dynamic, unfolding model of revelation! The book and angelic activity, coupled with the restoration of the priesthood and its attendant gifts, suggest also that the greatest days of the Restoration are just before us—when we shall see a nation born at once and a kingdom in a day.[3]

Our salvation cannot be considered separate, nor apart from, the restoration of God's ancient covenant people, the house of Israel. The subject of the gospel and that of the gathering of Israel being so connected, it is difficult to speak of one without mentioning the other.[4] This book is the covenant sent forth to recover His people, which are of the house of Israel.[5]

May the Book of Mormon—like the mustard seed—be found growing in the lives of the scattered Saints, that the angels may come and lodge in our branches, offering divine assistance to heal the breach and complete the work.

---

*Take away the Book of Mormon and the revelations, and where is our religion? We have none.*[6]

---

3    Isaiah 66:8.
4    *Latter Day Saints' Messenger and Advocate*, Vol. 1, No. 5, p. 109, Kirtland, Ohio, December 1835.
5    D&C 39:3e [39:11], B of C 41:10. Received in January 1831.
6    *The Latter-Day Saints' Millennial Star*, Vol. 19, p. 123, Quote from Joseph Smith, Jr., Edited & Published by S. W. Richards, Liverpool, England, 1857.

§

### The Angel Message and the Latter-day Light

*Yea, and he has made these things known unto us beforehand,
because he loveth our souls as well as he loveth our children; therefore
in his mercy he doth visit us by his angels that the plan of salvation
might be made known unto us as well as unto future generations. O
how merciful is our God![7]*

### Sara Jane Lively May
### The Reorganized Church of Jesus Christ of Latter Day Saints

I was born at London, Ontario, Canada, in the year 1853; and during the year 1866 my parents lived at Prairie Siding, near Chatham, Ontario. One day during that year, my mother and I were alone in the house, when someone came and knocked at our door and asked my mother if he might come in. He said that he was a messenger sent of God to teach us the way of life. We invited him in; and he told us that the true faith had been restored to the earth, that the true church with the fullness of the gospel and the gifts and blessings such as were enjoyed by the Church of Jesus Christ in His day and time was again established on the earth—and that this gospel was to be preached in all the world as a witness to all nations, and then shall the end come.

The beautiful gospel was made so clear and plain to us, such as we had never heard before. As he told the gospel story, we wondered and marveled at his great knowledge of the purposes and designs of God, which were to come to pass in this, the last dispensation of the fullness of times. He then arose, making ready to leave, when he turned to my mother and said that he desired to tell us some things that would assure us that the things he had told us were true, and for us to remember this prophecy: that during the year 1870 a war would come to pass between two great nations of Europe, and a king would be overpowered and would lose his throne. We took careful note of that which he told us, and just four years later, war broke out between France and Prussia.

7    Alma 14:38 [24:15].

Napoleon was defeated and lost his power; and thus, the prophecy truly came to pass.

He also told us that the day would come when we would hear this gospel preached and that all of the members of our family would become members of the Church of Jesus Christ about which he had spoken. We followed him to the door to get a last look at him; and behold, he was lost to our sight. We knew of no other person who had seen such a one as he, and we were reminded of the statement of Paul the apostle, wherein he said, "*Be not forgetful to entertain strangers; for thereby many have entertained angels unawares.*"[8]

Six years following the fulfillment of the prophecy concerning the war of 1870, while we were visiting with friends in London, Ontario, servants of God came preaching the gospel of the kingdom. As stated by the messenger sent to us, it was the same glorious fundamentals of truth, the same plan of salvation as that which was given to the Saints when our dear Lord dwelt here upon the earth among the children of men.

After we heard a few sermons preached by Elder J. J. Cornish, the Spirit said, "This is the way, walk ye in it." Therefore, I asked for baptism on Wednesday night December 29, 1875, at the close of a prayer meeting over which Elder J. J. Cornish had presided. Twenty members and ten nonmembers went down to the River Thames to attend the baptism of myself and another lady [Miss Polly Taylor]. It was about ten o'clock when we reached the bank of the river. It was extremely dark that night; so dark that we were not able to see each other. I had a great desire to be baptized first. Suddenly, as Brother Cornish stepped into the water, there descended from above a pillar of light, circular in shape, taking in the portion of the river where the baptism was taking place, and encircling those who were standing on the bank of the river. The light had come down from above as a mighty rushing wind. It was above the brightness of the noonday sun, and the Holy Spirit was poured out upon us in great

---

8    Hebrews 13:2.

power from on high. Our hearts were filled with great peace and joy, and we praised and glorified God for this marvelous manifestation of His love and power.

All were kneeling and thanking God for this blessing save the man who had been laughing and making fun. And a voice spoke to him saying, "These are my people. Do not laugh at them." Then the man turned to Brother Depper and asked him who it was that had spoken. But it was only he, William Clow, the one who had been making fun, who heard the voice. Later, Brother Clow and all his family joined the church.

This pillar of light continued to shine upon us and make clear the water of the flowing river until after the two of us were baptized. And as Brother Cornish stepped out of the water, the light began to ascend gradually until it went out of sight, leaving our hearts filled with an inexpressible joy and our souls aflame with the Spirit of God.

All the nonmembers present that night became members of the church. The statement made by the angel to me and my mother, that she and all her family would enter into the gospel fold, has been fulfilled as all her family and all her grandchildren have been baptized into the church.[9]

------------

*And they are as the angels of God, and if they shall pray unto the Father in the name of Jesus, they can show themselves unto whatsoever man it seemeth them good; therefore great and marvelous works shall be wrought by them, before the great and coming day, when all people must surely stand before the judgment seat of Christ.[10]*

------------

9   The Light on the River—>Centerplace.org (Menu: Library—>Testimonies—> The Light on the River.
10   3 Nephi 13:42–43 [28:30–31].

# 22

# Flying Above The Storm

*O Lord, give us strength according to our faith, which is in Christ, even unto deliverance.*[1]

Did you know that an eagle knows when threatening weather is approaching long before it breaks? The eagle will fly to some high spot and wait for the winds to come. When the storm hits, it sets its wings so that the wind will pick it up and lift it high above the disturbance. While the tempest rages below, the eagle is soaring high above it, gliding with ease. The eagle does not escape the portentous climate; it just simply uses the storm to lift it higher. It rises on the winds that bring the storm into its world.

Under the inspiration of the Holy Spirit, Joseph Smith, Jr., made some prophetic emendations to the Biblical text, illumining our <u>understanding.</u> One such prophetic correction referred to His Saints as

1    Alma 10:77 [14:26].

eagles:

*And now I show unto you a parable. Behold, wheresoever the carcass is, there will the eagles be gathered together; so likewise shall mine elect be gathered from the four quarters of the earth.* [2]

As the storms of conflict, antagonism, and obstruction come against the Restoration—and all of us have experienced these—we can rise above the storm by setting our minds and faith toward the promises of the latter-day theme, Zion. The storms do not have to overcome us. We can allow God to lift us above them as we find opportunity to unite with fellow believers. God can enable us to ride above the winds of opposition that have blown upon the Saints—that have brought so much division into the lives of the Scattered of the Restoration. The same winds that have brought pain, tragedy, failure, and disappointments in the work can be used by God to lift us above the storm like the eagle—causing something good to come from it.

It is not the disappointments of life, but it is how we handle them that counts. Nephi, of course, had suffered many privations. His family journeyed in the wilderness with periods of hunger, thirst, fatigue, and danger. He also had to deal with the contention created by his brothers, Laman and Lemuel, culminating in the division of their colony and ultimately war and bloodshed. In the face of all these privations and difficulties, Nephi was able to say:

*It came to pass that we lived after the manner of happiness.* [3]

Do we live under the manner of happiness? Nephi understood that there is a pattern for living that results in happiness, independent of the difficulties, challenges, frustrations, and setbacks that come into our lives individually and the church collectively—happy nevertheless. Nephi understood that the atonement would take place, and he had confidence that it would include both him and his people.

The Book of Mormon offers to the Saints a simple yet terribly

2    Matthew 24:28, IV.
3    2 Nephi 4:43 [5:27].

profound Christology centering in the atonement of the Lord Jesus, enabling the recipients of this book to apply the power of the atonement in our daily lives and (like the eagle) receive strength and deliverance throughout the storms of life. As possessors of and believers in this authentic ancient American artifact, we also are identified as eagles— those whom He will gather together to complete His work.

---

*Why not speak of the atonement of Christ, and attain to a perfect knowledge of him?[4]*

§

## Olive Oil

*Is any sick among you? let him call for the elders of the church; and let them pray over him, anointing him with oil in the name of the Lord; and the prayer of faith shall save the sick, and the Lord shall raise him up; and if he have committed sins, they shall be forgiven him.[5]*

### Brother Neil Simmons
### The Reorganized Church of Jesus Christ of Latter Day Saints

Having been assigned to develop the work of the church in northern Mexico, I had the privilege of working with a number of members and standing priesthood in that area. One of our members, a handicapped woman, told me of a small village in the interior of Mexico where she had been going during the winter and sharing her testimony. She repeatedly asked me to go to this small village and share the gospel. So in the course of events, I took a local elder with me and made the journey with her to this small indigenous village.

Arriving about dark, I was introduced to the local Protestant pastor. He found us a place to sleep for the evening. While we were unpacking

---

4    Jacob 3:18 [4:12].
5    James 5:14–15.

the car, a young woman rather hesitantly came up to me and asked if I would go pray for her husband. I explained that we follow the scriptural direction, anointing with consecrated olive oil, and laying on of hands, lifting up to God in prayer the one who is sick.

She was very agreeable and continued to press me for prayers for her husband. I asked my fellow priesthood member if he had brought his oil. He said that he did not have his oil with him. At the same time, I recognized that I had changed clothes and had left my small vial of oil at home. In some quandary, I thought that it might be permissible to just lay on hands and not use consecrated oil; but the thought died immediately because I knew that I had not tried to find any oil.

I explained to the young woman that I would go to town and get oil to consecrate for her husband and that we would shortly return for the prayer. I drove into the town; but it was after 10:00 p.m., and every little grocery place was already closed. My companion kept saying that we would not be able to find oil at this time of night, and we should just go back and offer prayer. But I persisted, driving up and down darkened streets, searching for some little shop that was still open—and silently praying for guidance from our Lord.

Up ahead, I could see a light on in a small store. I stopped and found it was a magazine shop, common in Mexico where paper and school supplies are sold. A bored young girl was sitting behind the counter when I walked in. I asked her if she had some olive oil, and she replied somewhat crossly in the negative. Standing there, I looked at the dusty shelves and the various magazine displays and repeated the question. Again, she said no oil. I replied that I was sure that she had some oil. At that point she cried out, *"Papá, aquí hay un hombre que me está fastidiando"* (Daddy, there is a man here bothering me).

A curtain moved in the back of the store, and briefly I could see living quarters behind the curtain; and then the owner was speaking— asking me why I was bothering his daughter. I replied that I wanted to buy some olive oil, and I was certain that it was available in his store. He shook his head in the negative and then stopped. He motioned his daughter to go out through the curtain. Then turning back to me, he asked why I wanted the oil. I explained it was for a prayer.

Without any further conversation, he got a small stepladder out, climbed up, looked through the shelves, and said *"No hay nada aquí"* (There is none here). I told him to look on top of the shelves. He climbed up until he could run his hand over the top of the shelves and repeated that there was nothing up there. I said to check in the top back corner "right over there," pointing to the place that I felt directed to tell him. He got down, moved the ladder, and tried again.

That time, he grunted, *"Aquí está"* (Here it is), and came down with an old small tin of virgin olive oil. As he climbed down, he said *"Ni yo sabía que estaba ahí"* (I didn't even know it was up there).

I was elated. I asked him for the price, and to my recollection he simply gave it to me for prayer. Returning to the village at about midnight, we went to the home of the woman who had requested prayer for her husband. When I got there and looked at him, I was shocked at how terribly bruised and cut he was. He was lying on a small cot, with only a pair of shorts on; and his body had bruises and cuts all over his arms and torso. I asked what happened. He groaned, saying his ribs hurt, and then explained that the bull he was trying to put into the corral had broken loose and had attacked him. It had ground him into the dirt, and thrown him like a rag doll all over the corral until help had come to distract the bull and rescue him.

We anointed him with the consecrated olive oil and prayed for him. After offering condolences and seeing that we could do nothing more for him, we went back to our little house and to bed.

The next morning I explained that we would have to leave so I could be home in time for church services. But before we left, I wanted to go see the young man who was so terribly beaten by the bull.

As we walked through the village toward the little house where we had last seen the wounded man, I noticed that there was someone in the corral with the bull. As we got closer, that person saw me. Running toward me, he jumped over the rail and presented himself to me. "*¡Estoy sano!*" (I am healed!), he shouted with what can only be described as joy. His wife ran out of the house and began thanking us profusely. We had to explain again to her that her thanks, and his, should be to the God of heaven.

It probably does not surprise anyone that in the coming months we were able to baptize more than twenty adults in that small village. I have never again questioned whether I could substitute an emblem used in an ordinance and have it approved by God. It was clear to my mind that He wanted me to use the proper anointing and He provided for it according to our faith.[6]

---

# Commentary

When Jesus built His church, He placed within it various helps and governments. Our tradition of the use of consecrated olive oil is one of those helps. The use of consecrated oil by the elders has a long and storied tradition among the Saints. Each branch of the Restoration can testify of its efficacy. There is, of course, no magical or special power in the olive oil. But when consecrated by the elders through the prayer of faith, it becomes a symbol recognized by God of the outpouring of the Holy Spirit, as well as an object for the exercise of our faith. It reminds us to have our lamps trimmed and burning, with oil (the Holy Spirit), that we may be ready at the coming of the Bridegroom. Just as surely as the power of God was manifest in the healing of the man gored by the bull, so, too, can God heal the breach in the Restoration. May we all sense and feel the anointing of the Holy Spirit in our lives, that the

---

6    Personal letter to the author.

healing may begin among the Scattered of the Restoration, that we, too, can together proclaim, "*¡Estamos sanos!*" (We're healed!).

---

*And thou shalt command the children of Israel that they bring thee pure oil olive beaten for the light, to cause the lamp to burn always.*[7]

---

7    Exodus 27:20.

# 23

# Spring Water

*For, lo, I will command, and I will sift the house of Israel among all nations, like as corn is sifted in a sieve, yet shall not the least grain fall upon the earth.*[1]

Have any of you ever had a bottle of spring water? More than half of the bottled water sold in the USA is labeled this way. Only a fraction of this water actually flows from a spring. The majority of this type of water is pumped from underground reservoirs. When it rains, water runs down the pavement into a ditch or patch of grass where some of it soaks into the ground. When this happens, it infiltrates the permeable soil and makes its way through the spaces between the rocks, sand, and other particles in the dirt. Eventually it collects in porous soil that has become saturated; all of its holes become filled with water. These layers are called aquifers. Some of these aquifers are hundreds of miles long, while others are quite small.

---

1    Amos 9:9.

Unlike surface water collected in rivers, lakes, and ponds, ground water is often quite clean and ready to drink. This is because the soil actually filters the water. The soil can hold onto the pollutants—such as living organisms, harmful chemicals, and minerals—only letting the clean water through.

When God scattered former-day Israel and sifted them among the Gentiles, He did so specifically to preserve and purify them to be gathered back to Him in the latter days. Following the death of Joseph Smith, Jr., the Lord again performed a scattering—this time to preserve and ultimately purify both the Saints and His Church. The various Restoration churches have been collecting the Saints that were sifted among the Gentiles to cleanse them from false doctrine and the tenants of men manifested in general Christianity. The various churches of the Restoration—in spite of their differences—have all assisted in restoring men to a knowledge of the covenants made with Israel, instructing them in the doctrine of Christ, and washing away their sins in the waters of regeneration. These churches are God's spiritual aquifers, holding the Saints until He makes bare His arm, when He will bottle them all under the same label.

———————

*And after they had been received unto baptism, and were wrought upon and cleansed by the power of the Holy Ghost, they were numbered among the people of the church of Christ.*[2]

§

### The Book Is True

As I read, the spirit of the Lord was upon me, and I knew and comprehended that the book was true, as plainly and manifestly as a man comprehends and knows that he exists.[3]

———————

2   Moroni 6:4.
3   *Autobiography of Parley P. Pratt*, pp. 36–37, Deseret Book Company, Salt Lake City, Utah, 1985.

## Brother Clayton Christensen
## The Church of Jesus Christ of Latter-day Saints

Clayton Christensen had already served a two-year mission to Korea and thought he was certain of his beliefs. But he wanted to have an absolute knowledge of the truthfulness of the Book of Mormon. Each night at eleven, he would kneel down and pray to God for a testimony. After praying, he sat and read one page, and then he stopped and thought about what he had read. Then he would kneel again, asking God to reveal the truthfulness of the Book of Mormon. Then he read another page. This discipline was carried on for many weeks.

He said, "One evening in October, 1975, as I sat in the chair and opened the book following my prayer, I felt a marvelous spirit come into the room and envelop my body. I had never before felt such an intense feeling of peace and love. I started to cry and did not want to stop. I knew then, from a source of understanding more powerful than anything I had ever felt in my life, that the book I was holding in my hands was true."[4]

## Brother Raymond D. Zinser
## The Reorganized Church of Jesus Christ of Latter Day Saints

One of the most dramatic and meaningful spiritual experiences of my life was directly connected with reading the Book of Mormon. Prior to entering the U.S. Navy when I was 19 years old, I had not read the Book of Mormon from cover to cover. I had only read some of the chapters at random. Certainly the risks and hazards I faced as a command pilot of a blimp in World War II gave me more than enough incentive to turn to God and the Scriptures for strength and survival.

I decided to spend all my extra time studying the Book of Mormon until I had read every word and underlined key scriptures. In my squadron responsibilities, I was on a rotation of one day of flight, one day of duty

---

4    "When Giants Fall: What Business Has Learned from Clayton Christensen," *The New Yorker*, May 14, 2012.

and one day off. I could read all day on my day off and into the evening, and even on my duty day there were a few hours available which I could devote to reading. I had a private room in the flyers' quarters so I could read without interruption during my time off.

It took me 30 days to complete the book, which was the exact amount of time I had in an outlying base. Beginning with the first day and continuing through to the last day of reading the Book of Mormon, dramatic circumstances surrounded the reading. The power of the Spirit of God was strong and pervasive in my room. Whenever I walked out the door, the Spirit was no longer felt. But it immediately filled my entire being and consciousness when I stepped back over the threshold.

I marveled at the magnitude of the power, the awesomeness of the word of Christ operating in ancient America and the dramatic quickening of my mind and spirit. I looked forward with the highest anticipation to each day when I could continue my reading. The Spirit operated within the confines of my room. I didn't know how long the pattern would persist, but I knew that it continued each day in exactly the same manner. The Spirit would leave me at the door of my room and then engulf me again when I returned to the room. It became apparent after a few days that this pattern would continue if I continued faithful and diligent in my study of the book.

As I write this testimony, the Spirit once again confirms to me with power and assurance that the Book of Mormon is true, that Jesus is the Christ, and that Zion will come to pass prior to the return of Jesus.[5]

*Now behold, this is the testimony which is in me.*[6]

---

5    Raymond D. Zinser, Ph.D., *Recent Book of Mormon Developments*, Vol. 2, p. 157, Zarahemla Research Foundation, Independence, Missouri, 1992.
6    Alma 5:23 [7:13].

# 24

# Prophetic Whisperings

There are a myriad of ways in which the Holy Spirit has enlightened the people of God. One of these avenues is manifest through prophecy. Many such oracular experiences are referenced in scripture and have also been a rich part of our latter-day Saint legacy. This gift has offered divine direction to bless, guide, and sustain His Saints. It continues to be an integral part of the latter-day Saint milieu. Shared experiences dating back to antiquity have had the power to combine hearts, creating an inseparable bond. Like the ancient craft of attaching objects together with a needle and thread, so, too, can prophetic sutures manifest in the gifts of the Spirit fasten God's Saints together to complete our divine task.

The great American poet laureate Robert Frost wrote about two roads which diverged in a yellow wood and how the traveler looked down one—then choosing the other declared how it, "has made all the difference." Choosing a particular path in the woods or a fork in the road are ancient and deep-seated metaphors for life that cry out for a decision. Apostle Joseph Luff, from the Reorganized Church, tells of a time when he was walking over the countryside, and he came to a fork in the road. He stopped, looked both ways, and wondered which way to go. One way looked more traveled than the other, so he decided to take that road. He walked and walked, but seemed to get nowhere.

Then he knelt and asked God which direction he should go. The Lord replied, "My son, why didn't you ask Me up at the fork?" I would have told you which of these roads to take. Go back and take the other one."[1]

---

1   *True Restoration Testimonies*, compiled by Clara Thomas, p. 40, Sionita School, Inc., Bates City, Missouri, 1993.

The experiences that follow invite the Saints to take the path that will make all the difference.

§

# Gather Together in One

## Revelation Received by Clarence Wheaton
## The Church of Christ (Temple Lot)

Verily, I say unto you, My children, who have taken upon you the name of Mine only begotten Son, Jesus Christ, I have watched over you and preserved you for a wise purpose in Myself. As I have said unto you in times past that I should make known unto you your duty toward your brethren, therefore, I am pleased with the efforts that you have put forth and now make known unto you that this is your work—to gather together in one all those of My sheep who are scattered upon the face of the earth. Ye shall lay aside all contention with **your brethren of the different branches of My Church**, for in the day that I shall come to My temple, I will perfect them in theory and in doctrine, and in all things pertaining to My church. Ye shall continue to strive for a unity of My children that ye may in this way be better prepared to meet the world when you go out among them to preach the fullness of My gospel.[2]

# Hold It High

## A Dream Received by Sister Helen Tisler
## The Church of Jesus Christ (Bickertonite)

I asked the Lord how He looked upon the other factions of the Restoration and received this dream after visiting the Temple Lot group in Independence, Missouri, with Apostle Joe Calabrese and his wife.

---

2    *Zion's Advocate* Vol. 2, No. 8, p. 12, Church of Christ Temple Lot, Independence, Missouri, September 15, 1925 (emphasis added).

I saw a long building with several rooms. All were working, preparing some special work such as music, organization, etc., etc., but my attention was drawn to the roof of this building such as this:

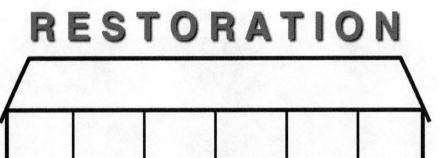

A voice then spoke to me, handing me a
lighted torch, and said, "Hold it high!"[3]

---

## Eating from the Same Dish

### Sister Minnie Kennedy
The Church of Jesus Christ (Bickertonite)

I had a dream that we were in a church building and Brother N. F. was preaching. After the meeting and before we left our seats, sisters on each side of me said, "What a grand sermon that was!" We went into another part of the building, and we all ate from the same dish. Those sisters that had sat by me during the service had been of the Reorganized Church and the Mormon Church, showing me again where the true church is and that we will someday all become as one people before God.[4]

---

3    *Heritage Series*, No. 21, "Hold It High," Published by Patrick S. McKay, Sr., Independence, Missouri, August 13, 2013..
4    Personal letter to the author.

# Just Like Minnie Kennedy

**Sister Becky Tarbuk**
**The Church of Jesus Christ (Bickertonite)**

I was traveling with a friend of mine to Hogensburg, New York, to attend a gathering on the Mohawk Indian Reservation. Approximately ten of us met for lunch at a restaurant. All were members of the Church of Christ (Temple Lot) except me. The waitress took our orders. Afterwards, one of the women in our group (who was the owner of the restaurant) asked the waitress to bring corn soup for us all to try—it being an old Indian soup recipe. Shortly thereafter, the waitress returned with two dinner-sized bowls of soup with two stacks of soup spoons. One bowl was set on each end of the table, and we were all encouraged to try it. As those of us on our end dipped into the soup, I gasped and said, "We're eating from the same dish just like Minnie Kennedy's experience." My friend Deb knew of the experience and encouraged me to tell Sister Minnie's dream. When I did, tears ran down the checks of the sister who ordered the soup.

She said, "How much more significant that it was Indian soup, as we will one day take the gospel back to the Indian people."

146

My father always said, "Only God can fulfill a dream." I believe this experience was a sign and confirmation that one day in the not too distant future we (the Scattered of the Restoration) will, indeed, eat from the same dish.

On Sunday afternoon, July 28, 2013, I was asked to share my recent experience of eating from the same dish. As I said, "And some day we will once again eat from the same dish," the word of the Lord came forth as follows:

> Hear My words now My people; hear My words now. I hear you speak this day, and I know your hearts this day, and I know your desires. And yes, the day will come when all My sincere believers will be brought back under one Shepherd, under one gospel, under one sound. It is the sound of My Son Jesus Christ. For He is the one Who came, and He lived in the flesh. He bore the sins of the world that He would be a testimony of My glory.

> And now you see in your day and time His return. You will see in your day and time as He, the Deliverer, will come back and He will unite His people again. He will unite them. And yes, records will come forth; they will confirm all the good things that I have given unto My people through all ages of time, and you will see My promises fulfilled.

> Rejoice in your day now; rejoice in your day. For great are the things that are before you! Open your hearts; open your minds; allow yourself to be used. For I have chosen instruments in these latter days, that they would do a work for me, a great work for Me; and you will all see My glory. Thus saith the Lord.[5]

---

5    Personal letter to the author.

# The Same Woman

### Brother Bill Leutzinger
### The Restoration Branch Movement

I attended the Zarahemla Branch on October 23, 2012, to hear an evangelist from The Church of Jesus Christ preach. That night after going to bed, I had the following dream: I saw a woman tall and stately, and she had the word "LAW" written over her chest. I immediately understood she represented the Reorganized Church of Jesus Christ of Latter Day Saints [Josephites].

I looked and again saw a woman clothed in gray clothes, somewhat bent over and humble. She had written across her chest the word "CUSTODIAN." I understood she represented the Church of Christ [Temple Lot].

I again looked and saw a woman, with the word "LOYALTY" written across her chest and realized she represented the Church of Jesus Christ of Latter-day Saints [Mormon Church].

Once again I looked and beheld a woman, and she had the words

"MANY GIFTS" written over her chest. I was made to understand she represented The Church of Jesus Christ [Bickertonites].

When I awoke, I shared the dream with my wife who responded, "Oh, it is like the pieces of a puzzle. All of these different women will get together."

I said, "No, they all represented the same woman with different characteristics."[6]

---

# Putting The Parts Back Together

**Dream of Brother Chuck Smith**
**The Church of Jesus Christ (Bickertonite)**

When we came to Oak Grove, Missouri, for the first time, we stayed for six weeks. In a dream I found myself under a car. Everything underneath the car—the transmission, the rear end, etc.— was all taken apart, and the parts were all in little piles under the car. My father, Isaac Smith (an apostle of this church), was standing outside

---

6    Related this experience to the First Quorum of Restoration Seventy, Independence, Missouri, April 2014.

the car telling me how to put these parts back together so the car could be operable again. I knew that the motor was just like new. It had not been used very much.

I got to thinking that—especially from the time of Joseph Smith's death—that spiritual car, or the church, was taken apart. My hope has been, like in this dream, one day the Saints will get back together again, and they will be one large body of people—you might say—singing praises to God. That is my hope. That is one reason I am out here in Missouri.[7]

---

# Three Dreams

## Sister Barbra Jordison
## The Restoration Branch Movement

During the early months of 2013, I was much concerned over things I heard and witnessed between Saints within various Restoration factions. I had been praying for oneness within the Restoration and knew the only answer to what separates us could be found in wisdom from the Lord. I had been praying the Lord would make clear to each person and group how they might find a way to work together. In the early hours of April 27, I received three separate dreams, awakening after each one. As I have never before received dreams in this manner and seldom recalled a dream with such clarity, the next morning I wrote them down.

### Dream One—The Gem

A small brown box, faded and worn from handling and broken at one corner, was shown to me. It was a size that could fit in the palm of a hand. I was made to know that factions of the Restoration had done this. Inside was a glorious gem that the Lord had given to the Restoration, sizable with a distinct cut and displayed on a radiant white

---

7    Related to the author in an email from Becky Tarbuk of The Church of Jesus Christ (Bickertonite).

setting. Instead of spending energy on sharing the beauty of the gem, the Restoration had become caught up in haggling over the packaging and presentation of it—so much so—that the small box in which it was originally presented had become overly worn.

These actions had diminished the opportunity for the precious stone's beauty and radiance to be seen. I then heard the scripture read which says, "*All tables are full of vomit and filthiness, so that there is no place clean.*"[8] I was given to know that if the Restoration would focus on the gem and cease all squabbling over the box, the Lord would allow them to continue to present the full radiance of the gem.

While I was later asked who was meant by the "Restoration," my understanding was that it meant heirs to the Restored Gospel, and that there is enough filthiness throughout—that none of us are standing in the clear light that we could be. We would be better served looking to our own righteousness.

### Dream Two—The Armada

I was shown an unpainted boat bobbing along in the water. Its sides were about eight inches thick, and the boat was large enough to hold about 12 to 15 large men. I could see that it was afloat without mast, rudder, oars or even oar rings. A leak in the side, near the bottom, could easily have been plugged. One man placed a white rag in the hole, which seemed to work for a short time, but another yanked it out, declaring, "You don't have the authority to do that." I could then hear three other men discussing how to plug the hole, and they eventually did. It, too, appeared to be working until someone else ripped it out, declaring, "You haven't done things in the proper order."

Meanwhile, the water level in the boat was rising (almost to waist level) as arguments continued about how best to plug the hole, and the rag was replaced and then tugged away by one after another.

---

8    Isaiah 28:8.

I was then taken to a vantage point far above the boat, where I could see a sizable armada of vessels and ships of many different types—some pristine and magnificent in size, others more humble—but all moving together in a unified direction.

As I noticed the unpainted boat previously mentioned, I saw that it was lagging toward the rear of the armada, slowing its pace in comparison with the others. I was given to know this boat represented the Restoration Movement. I heard a voice say, "These were the first laborers in this last kingdom." I was given to know that each boat in this armada belongs to the Lord and has been called to do the will of the Father.

It may seem unclear whom is meant by "first laborers." This phrase was used in the Doctrine and Covenants in 1832. I can only say that my sense from the dream was that this includes those in 2013.

### Dream Three—The Warriors

I was shown a single warrior, bare-chested, wearing a simple headband with a cloth that extended from his waist halfway down to his knees, with cloth leggings wrapped around his calves. In his hand he held a long and straight staff two and a half to three inches in diameter with a spearhead on the end. Sometimes he used it to push things aside, sometimes to draw things to him, and sometimes as a tool to spear things. Sometimes he held it in both hands and other times carried it at one side. It was a useful tool as long as it remained in his possession.

I observed that he was walking through tall grass, occasionally passing a tree. As I was able to look down upon a more expanded scene, I saw that he was walking in the same direction as other warriors—each dressed in the same way and each carrying the same type of spear. After a while, I noticed some of the men began poking the points of their spears at one another, puncturing and afflicting one another in the legs—wounding and causing them to bleed superficially. Some were

152

irritated at the pace of those before them. Others felt crowded by those walking next to them. Still others became impatient with those nearby and increased the distance between them. They spent so much time scrapping and wounding one another, they lost awareness of the terrain over which they were traveling; and they lost all true forward progress.

I was then given to know these warriors represented factions of the Restoration and that their behavior toward one another—putting each other down and minimizing the role and importance of the others—was a filthy stench before the Lord that He had grown weary of, so much so that I was shown the words "FILTHY STENCH" in capital letters.

I then saw Jesus, robed and standing atop a large stone. As each warrior stepped forward to raise a complaint about the methods and procedures of the others before the Lord, He pointedly said, "Lay it down." Over and over again, as each one came forward to validate his complaint with reasoning, the Lord would tell him emphatically to "Lay it down." He showed no interest in hearing what they had to say. As still they raised objections to one another, the Lord then fearsomely, forcefully, and slowly (pausing after each word) said, "NOT ONE WORD."

I was told to hear and understand—that if this band of brothers did not immediately end all complaints against one another, the Lord would remove Himself irrevocably from their midst. I was given to understand that every man, woman, and child who spoke as if to prefer themselves over another in any way emitted a horrible, filthy stench and would be banned from the presence of the Lord. I was then given to know that the only answer needed by the Restoration was to be still and prefer God's voice over their own.[9]

---

9    *The Latter Day Saints' Beacon*, Vol. 5, Issue 5, pp. 14–15, Joint Conference of
     Restoration Branches, Independence, Missouri, 2013.

# The Woman at the Well

**Patrick S. McKay Sr.**
**The Restoration Branch Movement**

While I was in the field on a missionary trip in California in February of 2013, I sat down to reply to an email I had received from a member of The Church of Jesus Christ. In part, this is what was written:

> When I read John 4, I feel there is something very important recorded in the verses. I feel the stirring of the Spirit. If we liken this passage to our day and the Scattered of the Restoration, we can see ourselves upon the pages and how it is possible for God to work with all of us, bringing us along until the day when we have to step out in faith and worship Him in Spirit and truth.

Of course, this individual was referring to the different churches of the Restoration, suggesting that as Jesus our Lord not only conversed with His disciples, the Jews, but also with the Samaritan woman with whom the Jews had no dealings, He could in like manner also be speaking to different branches of the Restoration—even though they do not speak to one another.

I had, of course, read the 4th chapter of John many times, but had not done so lately. As I began to write, I felt the inspiration of the Spirit and was given insights regarding the woman at the well.

I saw couched in this story a prophetic allegory regarding the Church and the healing of the breach within the Restoration. The woman represented the church restored in the latter days. The people who first occupied the land of Samaria were the children of Israel (the Northern Kingdom). They were carried into bondage by Assyria. There was, however, a remnant left in Samaria. The woman at the well was an Israelite (she refers to "our father Jacob"), and I understood she is a type of the latter-day church, which was sown among the Gentiles.

The woman had had five husbands, Joseph Smith, Jr., Brigham Young, Joseph Smith III, Granville Hedrick, and William Bickerton.[10] Additionally, Jesus told her that she was living with one now, who was not her husband.

Jesus appears to the woman at the well and tells her if she will drink from Jacob's well, she will thirst again. But if she will drink from this well (meaning Christ), she will never thirst. I was shown this is the promise of the fountain of living waters, the spirit of prophecy and revelation, which will now nourish her (not the organizations to which she has been connected). When a baby comes forth, the placenta falls away, no longer being necessary.

I saw our present condition and realized that when signs and wonders come more fully upon the church and she begins to rise out of obscurity, the placenta will fall away—like hay, wood, stubble, and all that is not pure and holy. The woman who had been nourished in the different Restoration organizations or churches will now discard those

---

10    Joseph Smith, Jr. (Original Church), Brigham Young (LDS Church), Joseph Smith, III (The Reorganized Church) Granville Hedrick (Church of Christ, Temple Lot), William Bickerton (The Church of Jesus Christ).

organizations much like a newborn that is now free of the placenta. The true believers will once again have placed at their head a husband or a prophet like unto Moses, to lead her out of bondage into the kingdom of Zion as prophesied by Joseph Smith in the early days of the Church:

> Behold, I say unto you, The redemption of Zion must needs come by power; therefore I will raise up unto my people a man, who shall lead them like as Moses led the children of Israel, for ye are the children of Israel, and the seed of Abraham; and ye must needs be led out of bondage by power, and with a stretched out arm; and as your fathers were led at the first, even so shall the redemption of Zion be. [11]

A few days later I reread John 4 and continued reading into chapter five. Here is recounted for us the story of the Pool of Bethesda or the Pool of Mercy, where those who were sick, impotent, and lame, etc., waited for the stirring of the water by the angel, with the hope they might be the first into the pool and receive healing. The story is remarkable, and again I felt my understanding enlarge as I read the account.

There were five porches where these sick folk lay. Immediately I could see in my mind's eye once again the church from the days of Joseph Smith, Jr., through its remaining remnants (the five porches) with her lame, sick, and impotent in need of healing both in body and in spirit. Each church of the Restoration can claim blessings and healings from time to time, but as yet none of the churches has the strength or vitality to complete the work given to the Restoration. I realized the day would shortly come when the waters of Bethesda would again be troubled or stirred; but this time the healing would not be limited to the first one in the pool, but all those on the five porches would enter the Pool of Mercy and be restored.

---

11   D&C 100:3d–e [103:15–18] Received February 1834.

# 25

# Epilogue

*Behold, this I have given unto you a parable, and it is even as I am: I say unto you, Be one; and if ye are not one, ye are not mine.*[1]

Nephi retrieved the Brass Plates from Jerusalem, ascended the mount, built a ship, and sailed to the Promised Land—gaining momentum to forge a nation that would one day receive the Savior. At the end of the Nephite nation, Mormon and Moroni abridged the history of their people and quoted profusely from the Brass Plates as they created their own abridged history on a new set of plates, which would lay hidden in the earth for over 1400 years.

Joseph Smith, Jr., the Palmyra Seer, retrieved those plates containing that testimony, which initiated the Restoration with the commission to build the Holy City to which God's ancient covenant people would be gathered and prepared when the Savior returns to make up His jewels.

But Joseph was martyred, the church fractured, and the Saints scattered. Since that time, the various branches of the original church have magnified their differences—carving out competing and rival factions. These schisms have led to a variety of views regarding our shared history as well as our future. This collection of organizations represents the constellation of the Restoration, each of which today competes for ascendancy across the spiritual landscape of the Restored Gospel and its ideal of Zion. These branches jointly find that their strength is manifest in their adherence to both the Christology and its soteriology revealed in the Book of Mormon—which illuminates for us the justice and mercy of God as lived out through the principle of free will. But administrative differences and priesthood authority remain as

---

1    D&C 38:6a [38:27], BofC 40:22, *The Evening and the Morning Star*, Vol. 1, No. 8, p. 61, published January 1833, (received January, 1831).

the elephant in the room which keeps us separate. Our fragmentation has left us twisted and caught in a snare. Zion finds herself in bondage, a complicated situation or circumstance from which she yearns to be free.

Our histories are all so very important, having shaped and fashioned our views regarding the latter-day work. Former Prime Minister of Great Britain, Winston Churchill once said:

If we open a quarrel between past and present, we shall find that we have lost the future.[2]

In our effort to faithfully declare the Restored Gospel, we have identified the flaws of all the other Restoration churches as we attempt to validate our own existence. Today a nascent landscape is emerging before us as we look to the future of a unified people building up the kingdom of God on earth. This monograph is inviting us to consider a new idea, to view the other branches of the Restoration in a fresh light. If we do, we will be amazed at what God has done to confirm the truthfulness of the work with others, similar to what He has done in our individual movements. It is now the time to close those quarrels and mend the breaches.

Sociologists tell us that the emphasis in identity conflict is on one's diversity. That applies to the various branches of the Restored Church and how these branches are different—whether one group or another is viewed to be superior or more right in their adherence to the gospel principles than another.

A couple of years ago an evangelist from The Church of Jesus Christ (Bickertonite) visited my home branch. He told a story about his son's dog, Radar. There was a privacy fence in the yard, which made it impossible for Radar to view the cars, buses, bicyclers, and various individuals passing by, so Radar would bark. He could not really see who was there, so he just barked at them.

One day Radar apparently got an idea to go into the house and look

2    https://en.wikiquote.org/wiki/Winston_Churchill

out a window, which was higher than the fence. All of a sudden he stopped barking. He could see what was on the other side of the fence, and he saw that these people were not really much different from those he was accustomed to seeing on his side of the barrier. Radar is quite an insightful dog from which we all could learn.

As I reflected on this account, a simple little tale came forcibly to mind. One day Alexander the Great came across the philosopher Diogenes. Diogenes was staring attentively at a heap of bones. "What are you looking for?" asked Alexander.

"Something that I cannot find," replied Diogenes.

"And what might that be?"

"The difference between your father's bones and those of his slaves."[3]

This anthology of metaphors and its attendant testimonies and commentary have attempted to magnify the wisdom and insight of this formerly barking canine, illustrating the value of looking over the walls that have divided the Saints since 1844 and discovering—like both Radar and Diogenes—that we're really not that different.

There are many Saints in the different branches of the Restoration who have remained faithful to the gospel as it has been delivered to them. It may have come to another a little differently, but we all share a portion of the latter-day light. The Saints in their scattered condition should applaud all efforts within the different churches of the Restoration which advocate and promote the divine authenticity of the Book of Mormon. Enemies abound, attempting to disannul the work by sowing doubt in the hearts and minds of the Saints. Casualties of the conflict have been realized in each portion of the Restoration with many Saints being deceived and overcome by the sophistry of men. Our scattered condition limits us from combining our knowledge, our resources, our gifts, our testimonies, and our faith to speak with one voice against the avalanche of unbelief and criticism of the angel message. There are

---

3    http://storiesforpreaching.com/category/sermonillustrations/dignity/

however, prodigious stores of gifts yet available to those who have an eye single to God's glory. Can we secure for ourselves those heavenly provisions which will grace our lives and enable us to become a united people, a people with a divine destiny?

Joseph Stalin, one of the most tyrannical and brutal leaders of all time, knew all too well that ideas could transform people, nations and empires. He warned:

Great ideas are more powerful than guns. We would not let our enemies have guns. Why should we let them have ideas?[4]

Have you ever had an idea that you hoped others might recognize, embrace, and help bring to fruition? President John F. Kennedy once declared:

A man may die, nations may rise and fall, but an idea lives on. Ideas have endurance without death.[5]

President Kennedy's words capture for me the hope I have of the possibility of the Saints becoming united. Yes, ideas can transform people. This book has proffered common testimonies, shared history, personal observations and poignant commentary on our latter-day Saint legacy, illustrating that God has been active in the lives of the Saints in the various churches of the Restoration.

There is the story of a little girl who was sweeping the floor of a room into which the sunlight was streaming through a large window. Looking up, she noticed that within the space where the streak of light crossed the room the dust was floating thickly. Going over to the window, she quickly drew the blinds down and darkened the room. When asked why she had done this, she replied that she wanted to exclude the sunlight because it made the room look dirty.

Through the window of our shared history, we have an abundance

---

4    *Quotations for Public Speakers: A Historical, Literary and Political Anthology,*
      p. 21, by former Senator Robert Torricelli, Rutgers Universtiy Press, 2000.
5    http://www.presidency.ucsb.edu/ws/index.php?pid=9551

of light to illumine our path. These streams of light both identify some of our flaws, and forecast a bright future and the dawning of a new day for the Scattered of the Restoration. May we be found employing the counsel of Rupertus Meldenius, an early seventeenth century German theologian:

> In things essential unity, in things nonessential liberty, and in all things charity.[6]

As we do so, the Saints will be encouraged to see and applaud all attempts within the different branches of the Restoration Movement which advocate and promote the divine authenticity of the Restored Gospel.

The purpose of this book is to persuade it readers to consider the degree to which the Holy Spirit has blessed the various portions of the Restoration Movement, with the hope that if God has recognized these various churches by pouring out His Spirit upon them, perhaps the Saints will acknowledge them as well. Jesus taught the Nephites to:

> *Ask and it shall be given unto you; seek, and ye shall find; knock, and it shall be opened unto you.[7]*

This same axiom applies to the Scattered of the Restoration. The path forward to become a united people, although difficult to apprehend, is assured within the pages of the book we all cherish:

> *And thus will I bring them together again, that they shall bring forth the natural fruit; and they shall be one.[8]*

Like Nephi, we, too, are looking for momentum—that force, impetus or driving power to catapult us into the future where we see a nation born at once and a kingdom in a day[9] when:

> The purposes of God shall be accomplished, and the Great Jehovah shall say the work is done.[10]

---

6    https://www.goodreads.com/author/quotes/4392934.Rupertus_Meldenius
7    3 Nephi 6:19 [14:7].
8    Jacob 3:134 [5: 68].
9    Isaiah 66:8.
10   Joseph Smith, Jr., *History of the Church* [LDS], Vol. 4, p. 540.

The reuniting of the Saints is not really a new idea. God has purposed from the beginning to gather scattered Israel, and He desires to do the same with the Scattered of the Restoration. It is as the poet has written:

Tale as old as time, song as old as rhyme.[11]

This can become the nexus of our common destiny, causing us to rejoice at the good He brings in these latter days. Let us labor shoulder to shoulder as we look forward with anticipation to that hour, which is fast approaching when we shall all see eye to eye as He brings again Zion.

Come Saints, build the old waste places,
Raise the old foundations high.
Then our heritage will find us,
And our song will fill the sky.

Repair the breach, restore the pathways,
Where our fathers walked so long.
Oh, loose the bands, the heavy burdens,
And lend the weary ones a song.[12]

# The *Beginning*!

---

11  Lyrics from *Beauty and the Beast*, written by Lyricist Howard Ashman, 1991.
12  Arlene Buffington, *The Songs of Zion*, Vol. 2. No. 210, "Lend the Weary Ones a Song," unpublished.

# Index

163

Enemies, 159, 160

Enemy, 3, 120

Ensign Balloon Corporation, 51

Entangled, 23, 24

Ephraim, 74

Evangelist, 148, 158

Evangelistic, 95

Evangelize, 98

Evans, R. C., 95, 96

Eve, 9

Everlasting, 24, 42, 45, 58, 66, 105, 121, 124

Explosion, 118

Eyeballs, 96

Eyelids, 19

# F

Fabric, 11, 29, 44, 115, 116

Fabrics, 115

Factions, 58, 144, 150, 153, 157

Faithful, 27, 41, 47, 48, 142, 159

Faithfully, 158

Fallen, 9, 63, 116

Families, 6, 39

Fashioned, 158

Fast, 18, 43, 44, 78, 95, 162

Fasted, 49

Fate, 42, 112

Fellowship, 5, 47, 82

Fellowships, 3

Felt, 2, 10, 12, 34, 37, 48, 59, 64, 77, 84, 85, 93, 115, 116, 122, 135, 141, 142, 152, 155, 156

Fiber, 115

Fibers, 115

Filthiness, 151

Filthy, 153

Flexibility, 81

Foaled, 41, 42

Focus, 81, 82, 151

Forecast, 24, 116, 161

Foreshadow, 42

Foretaste, 3, 82

Foretelling, 110

Foretells, 32

Foretold, 20, 110

Fortunate, 9, 10, 62

Fortune, 97

Fountain, 155

Fowler, Mary, 91, 94

Fox, Lowell, 106

Fractal, 89

Fractal–like, 89, 90

Fractaled, 90

Fraction, 139

Fractions, 3

Fractured, 58, 90, 157

Fractures, 62

Fragment, 62

Fragmentation, 158

Freed, 24

Friendship, 91

Friendships, 3, 82

Fruits, 45, 120, 121

Fulfilled, 129, 147

Fulfilling, 78

Fulfillment, 2, 128

Fullness, 33, 43, 78, 84, 121, 127, 144

Fundamental, 91

Fundamentals, 128

Furiner, Thurman. 48

# G

Garment, 35, 36, 97

Garments, 46, 76

Gathering, 15, 33, 37, 66, 68, 125, 126, 146

Gem, 150, 151

Generations, 6, 32, 63, 110, 127

Genetic, 31, 32

Gentile, 78

Gentiles, 77, 119, 140, 155

Geode, 45, 46

Geodes, 45

Geologists, 46

Golden Joinery, 61

Golden Repair, 61

Gonzales, Robert, 73

Goodwin, 19

Graft, 32, 120

Grafted, 11, 32, 119, 120, 124

Grafting, 10, 120

Grafts, 121

Grain, 139

Groups, 17, 32

# H

Haines, Deb, 12

Handicapped, 133

Happier, 46, 55

Happiness, 132

Healings, 18, 156

Heirs, 33, 46, 112, 151

Helium, 52

Henderson, "Sister" 19

Hensley, Elsie, 77

*Herald*, 29, 126

Hereditary, 31

Heritage, 5, 162

Historical, 32, 98, 116, 160

Histories, 20, 158

Horse, 26, 41, 42, 50

Horses, 41, 42

House of Israel, 3, 10, 32, 72, 74, 76, 78, 90, 110, 119, 121, 124, 126, 139

Humpback [whale], 23, 24

# I

Idea, 52, 58, 75, 90, 158, 160, 162

Ideal, 4, 157

Idealistic, 53

Ideas, 160

Illuminates, 86, 157

Illumine, 76, 161

Illumining, 131

Illustrated, 76, 98

Illustrating, 66, 121, 159, 160

Independence,  Mo. 53, 77, 111, 144

Indian, 146

Indians, 75, 76, 78

Indigenous, 133

Inez, 53

Inheritors, 42

Inseparable, 143

Insight, 159

Insightful, 159

Insights, 16, 155

Inspiration, 131, 155

Integral, 143

Interconnected, 1, 3

Interdependence, 2

Interdependent, 2, 15

Interlocking, 115

Interlocks, 115

Interpretation, 50, 59, 121

Isaac, 149

Isaiah, 4, 11, 17, 62, 63, 108, 112, 116, 122, 126, 151, 161

Israel, House of, 3, 10, 32, 72, 74, 76, 78, 90, 110, 119, 121, 124, 126, 139

Israelite, 155

Italian, 6, 7

Italy, 6

-ites, 46, 112

# J

Jehovah, 162

Jellyfish, 65

Jersey, 34, 35

Jerusalem, 5, 157

Jewels, 68, 157

Jiggling, 118

Joined, 6, 78, 110, 123, 129

Joinery, 61

Joining, 32

Jointly, 105, 157

Jordison, Barbra, 150

Josephites, 148

Jubilee, 111, 112

# K

Kennedy, Minnie, 145, 146

Kintsukuroi, 61, 62

Kirkpatrick, Clarence, 99

Kyriakako, Stephen, 43

# L

Labor, 29, 60, 162

Labored, 78

Laborers, 152

Laboring, 60, 102

Lamanite, Samuel the, 112

Lamanites, 78, 109

Lamar, Fred, 123

Lamar, Althea, 123

Landscape, 157, 158

Lasik, 81, 82

Latter–day, 2, 5, 11, 19, 20, 24, 25, 36, 44, 53, 58, 68, 83, 86, 98, 106, 116, 121, 127, 132, 141, 143, 148, 155, 158–160

Lehi, 9, 72, 112

Lens, 81

Leutzinger, Bill, 148

Lovalvo, Leonard, 6

Liberated, 24

Liberty, 24, 161

Linchpin, 109, 110

Loom, 19, 115

Luff, Joseph, 143

Luffman, Dale 113

# M

Magical, 136

Magnificent, 152

Magnified, 3, 157

Magnify, 159

Magnifying, 110

Magnitude, 142

Magnum, 74

# X

# Y

# Z

CPSIA information can be obtained
at www.ICGtesting.com
Printed in the USA
LVHW032213200120
644239LV00002B/360